Locate Yourself

Dorothy Simpson

Printed by JOP (Jeff Oliver Print) 24 Walton Street, Whangarei, NZ.

ISBN: 978-0-473-43459-5
ISBN: 978-0-473-45050-2 (E Publication)

Authors Note:

The content of this book is destined to be educational and empowering. It is not intended to be prescriptive in any way.

All information offered is for expanded awareness in regards to wellbeing and health care options. It should not be misinterpreted as a diagnostic and treatment tool.

Any ideas and suggestions contained in this book are not planned as a substitute for consulting with your physician. However it is advised to seek advice from several health and wellbeing professionals.

The author and publisher are in no way liable for any consequences of a reader failing to take appropriate advice from a health professional.

For my husband who gave me security when I needed it most,
I thank you.

For my children who are my healers, I leave this legacy for you.

For my grandchildren who are not manifested yet,
I leave this wisdom.

Contents

Section Four

Dear Reader,

Upon completion of this book I realised that there was an expectation to discuss my writing, my intended audience and comparable authors to this text. So now I will explain my writing to the reader who begins to travel through this tome.

My writing could be described as chunky not smooth. I liken it to a roller-coaster ride; it's constant, but has anticipated drops and moments of being jolted from side to side. That is not deliberate it's — just that the topics are many to match the multi-faceted human experience. The narrative is chatty. It bobs along with autobiographical snippets, often plummets into scholarly research, and enters mysticism when you least expect it.

The topics discussed are like a tour through a museum; each room has a quaint theme and no two rooms are similar, but the stairwells and corridors are smooth-cream-coloured linkages that assist the reader to roll out of one exploration room into another.

The audience is you because you are reading this. Yet at the beginning the concept was intended as an education manual for students undertaking humanities and health sciences studies. However I now believe there is a broad audience out there that includes; anyone who is curiously observant about how they hold space within themselves, and who feels at odds for some reason. My hope is that the reader will tell me how the text contributed to their wellbeing.

The text fits securely within self-help. Comparable authors and researchers are many, but not comparable to *Locate Yourself* within one tome. There are many authors who have contributed to my wellbeing and now I add a little bit of my flavour to this genre that concerns itself with mind, body and soul.

I hope this offers some explanation.

Blessings,

Dorothy

Locate Yourself

Introduction

Threads of pain and confusion weave themselves into stories within stories, lost in their uniqueness as a single thread — hidden, forgotten, unnoticed, obscured until the break, the unravelling begins.

Weaving fibres of any kind requires the weft and the warp to hold the foundation strong as you build the cloth.

This book encourages the reader to recognise the importance of knowing their beginning, and identify their beliefs about their thoughts, their health, and the patterns they carry forward into the legacy of their own children.

Like the weaving of cloth, our foundation needs to be strong. *Locate Yourself* is a guide to assess foundational scripts from pre-birth, family care and societal influence that mould an individual. When the foundation is harmful the cloth is weak and breaks, causing all manner of chaos and personal challenge.

To break an unhealthy cycle is to first recognise the signs of a defective foundation. Woven through this book is the author's story of abandonment, adoption, and the compounding damage that formed an unhealthy foundation to build social and intimate relationships on. The author reset her foundation and reformed her self-belief with knowledge from psychology, indigenous and mindfulness practices, spirituality and the personal need to understand her story to locate her authentic self.

Gathering knowledge alerted the author to the vastness of relevant, current research available to avert neglect and mismanagement of vulnerable people. Yet it also showed how the drive for credible research creates hazards for effective intervention. Research has parameters that narrow the confines of credibility because it often quantifies itself to percentage effectiveness and substantiated by peer-reviewed scientific literature, yet the evidence they strive to make an effective intervention from suggests that the human condition should be covered with a broadly targeted brush. This is like a fishing trawler dropping a big net to catch fish for high-demand markets. There are always the fish that don't get caught with intervention. They are too wary of the boat and the turbulent water to get close to the net. This is how people go under the radar of detection, avoiding early intervention or explanation.

Scholarly articles, research questioning and exploration are fundamentally important, fostering self-empowerment, ongoing transformational healing and recovery intervention that benefit many people. Yet self-directed enquiry is an equally important healer if it delivers clarity and understanding for even one individual. There is a scholarly war between scientific dogma and anecdotal narrative, and unfortunately this leads to the net not being able to gather the vulnerable and provide a one-fit-for-all explanation.

So I'd like to sound a warning to the scholars who struggle with how to substantiate individualised care plans that can seem purely philosophical without application for mass evidenced truths. I suggest that as you read this you let yourself get caught up in the whimsy and simplicity, since this self-directed exploration is angled at the disarranged fish that has avoided the net thus far.

As much as the author cherishes the direction that can be gained from reading thesis upon thesis on each topic mentioned within this book, it can't be said that every disarranged person has the same interest or understanding of the mass referencing of executive knowledge within psychology and health research.

My aim has been to deliver a simplified interpretation of research and narrative in a directory format. The level of investment is individual; anyone who feels a need to explore the material mentioned should gratify their interest with a Google search leading to library resources or professionals regardless of whether they are academically specialised, indigenous, or practitioners of alternative practices.

Humans have a beginning and an end, and stuff in between. "so who are you — a product of all the previous stuff"? The stuff varies for everyone. This book introduces the variants that could create a wobbly foundation and explains in easy-to-understand language how "the stuff" may impact an individual.

The four sections of the book offer knowledge as the tool of empowerment.

The first section suggests the importance of understanding your foundation and thinking about your belief system, and your behaviours. It sows the seed of breaking free of imposed family programming that is no longer benefiting you. It raises awareness about toxic parenting, attachment to a significant carer, co-dependency, post-traumatic stress disorder, social positioning, and the need to locate yourself, to re-create your foundation by pressing the delete button on stuff that doesn't honour your life moving forward.

The second section introduces the ecological model and explains that you are a valued part of something beyond the family. This section gives the individual permission to change and take their personal power back; it also explains key areas that hold you stuck in your story. It opens the reader to new terminology around family systems, culture and needs, along with the affirming language of hope, resilience and forgiveness, with the aim of becoming self-aware and giving yourself permission to reframe your personal beliefs.

The third section overviews personal health management, with an emphasis on identifying the tribe of helpers and healers, known and unknown. It explains the importance of the four quadrants of the self-assessment tool, separating the person into the biological, psychological, social and spiritual components within the quadrants to locate any imbalance. This visual tool forms the backbone of self-sorting. Instead of handing the power of diagnosis over to a medical professional, the reader can streamline and articulate information for a more accurate diagnosis.

The fourth section encourages the reader to define their wellness tools of choice, which may be an eclectic mix of knowledge gathered from Western and Eastern thinking. This section locates the tribe of people and things that form the helpers and healers mentioned in section three. Together they will support the individual, expanding and laying new foundational stones to locate who you are now.

Once the cloth is broken, given time a hole develops, and it can then be hard to find the initial threads that broke under strain. *Locate Yourself* is my gift to the resilient yet disarranged people to help them find the damaged threads that started their unravelling.

Plot Your Course

Locate Yourself introduces thought-provoking material. The four sections introduce concepts steeped in psychology and tools of self-care. The writing is self-help exploration. It can be frustrating to journey through a book and realise that you want to retrieve a piece of information, but you forgot where you read it. For this reason it is suggested that you keep a notebook to journalise any thoughts, experiences and ideas that present when you follow this writing.

There are diagrams and templates that offer structure and sequence. Make note of the page number where you found quotable content, or where you were triggered to a memory, feeling, emotion, or any "aha, so that is what it's called" or "I thought so" moments. By following this process your journal should unpack your story and help you make some sense of your patterns and choices in this lifetime.

Section One

First Impressions

Prelude

The purpose of living is to die knowing that you found joy, love, peace and anger, you celebrated, you mourned, you found yourself, you healed. And as you found yourself you guided others to make their selves whole, and they then continue the work of guiding people to locate their value. This is my work, and it originally started when I set out to heal the confusion of my birth and adoption scars, and ultimately find my belonging.

But you can't find yourself until you know you're lost.

Īna kei te mohio koe ko wai koe, i anga mai koe i hea, kei te moiho koe. Kei te anga atu ki hea.

If you know who you are and where you are from, then you will know where you are going.

Māori Proverb.

I found my voice in my teenage years when I realised I was reacting from being a victim of multiple injustices, unfairness, cruelty, and a lack of verbal and physical love from my adoptive parents.

Acting out in school from neglect and absent parenting perpetuated learning difficulty, like most kids who experience these issues — we develop strategies that morph us into inanimate fixtures because we are dumb, angry, frustrated, different, odd, challenged.

How did I begin to orientate the struggle?

Faith in a voice.

The voice came to me when I was around nine years old. The lead-up is blurred but I remember I was going to kill myself. For a young person, when hope is out of reach death looks attractive. I had decided to jump out the window in my parent's bedroom to end my existence; maybe I would be mourned, maybe understood, maybe loved, and maybe cherished.

Somewhere in my head came a voice saying, "If you die now you will have to come back and redo this life. It's your purpose to live this experience, endure this pain. All this emotional pain is only in your early life; your adult life will be okay. You have already lived nine years — if you die now your lesson is not learnt. Why go back and waste the present nine years of this childhood pain experience? This is the lesson you need to endure before you complete your reincarnation life cycle."

This memory was pivotal to my continuing to live. The maths was simple… adulthood to me was 18 years so I was already halfway. So I carried on living, breathing, enduring, often happy, most times content, mostly unloved in the way I needed to be loved.

My parents struggled with each other and didn't realise my needs. They missed the cues, and mine were easy to miss because I didn't act out — but I craved their love which often never came when I needed it.

Spirit Voice was correct: I have lived a blessed adulthood. I started the healing process by understanding that I didn't fit with people, I didn't trust people, I didn't attach to people, I had low self-worth, I felt I was a failure and I was still a victim of my childhood. I craved love and connectedness, yet I continually pushed people away.

The voice periodically returned to me in times of struggle; it came rarely, but every time the guidance was accurate.

The mix of intuitive guidance and knowledge brought me new learning perspectives:

- Exposure to different people showed me that my struggles dulled in comparison to different types of abuse endured by others.

- Relevant teachings and guidance crossed my path.

- Other people's input shaped my understanding that I was OK.

- I come from financial and emotional poverty.

- Social positioning gave me more advantages than people with physical disabilities, cognitive distortion, and skin colour.

- I was young and healthy.

- I had a plan, a goal-orientated brain, outward confidence with a sense of fun, and the desire to find my belonging.

My drive for security was paramount.

Turangawaewae… belonging… attachment… connection… secure in anchoring to something solid that couldn't be taken away from me by others in the game of life. I would be in control of that safe harbour. I was a free spirit, and that freedom allowed me to meet pivotal people who influenced me positively and negatively, but all times helped me to grow in understanding of who I was and who I wanted to be. I was developing the concept of my personal power, defining my boundaries and evolving my belief that the only thing you can change is yourself and your future… not your family… and not your past.

Past You
Yesterday and all the other
yesterdays are past

Present You
in the
NOW

Future You
Design
your legacy

Figure 1

Boundaries and Power

Personal boundaries are morphed from a combination of family and community rules, accepted conduct, ethnic belief, and individual subconscious survival criteria.

At any point in a person's life they can re-evaluate and question assimilated boundary beliefs.

In order to locate yourself within yourself you need to unpack your beliefs and actions. A person is always the collective influences of their history thus far; today is current, while yesterday and all the previous yesterdays are your history. If beliefs are weighted down over time, requiring justifications and energy to make them fit — especially if you think they are wrong... it becomes hard work making them fit in the now moment if new information offers an alternative belief.

Cognitive human development says a young adult develops their questioning voice, makes decisions based on their thinking — after questioning the whys and how comes. They learn to separate the self and identity from earlier collective influences — beginning a transformation of discovering their inner person who thinks differently from their childhood programming. An individual is born.

Growing and challenging their foundational beliefs allows the person to exercise independent thinking. They should develop individual reasoning ability and be able to double-check their thoughts with adults around them.

If their networks and parenting have been positive then all is good; they should have sound solid people to help guide decisions. If the parenting has been biased, abusive, neglectful, dictatorial or toxic; they could struggle to make good decisions because of deficit role models, and also lack trust in their own decision making. Emotional and/or physical power differentials can also cause delays in their autonomy process since they fear retribution from the people who are meant to care for them.

Breaking free from here is difficult and painful, but when completed the process can be powerful as the individual begins to voice their own thoughts, decisions, desires and dreams, without worrying about the opinions of key people who hold authority or obligation over their life.

Personal autonomous power develops naturally for some kids. Others have to steal it back from significant adults.

I had to steal my power back from my mother, my family members and my collective school experiences. I had to establish my self-esteem, my self-worth, and my self-control. It wasn't easy — it took eight years of being assertive, knocked down, ridiculed, excluded, exposed to a raft of abuses and humiliation — but I did it.

The person I became was the one who'd lain dormant inside me. The girl who wanted to be loved and cherished had to endure more hardship to become free of familial judgement. If I had not challenged that judgement it would have rendered me a puppet of false identity instead of an independent, autonomous, free-thinking, caring person. In other words a human doing — not a human being.

I wanted more for me. I needed to show people that I was this amazing human and I wanted to be emotionally healthy, not questioning the balance of human exchange within my family.

Revolving Door

This book came to me as an idea in late 2015 as I watched my teenage children and their friends grow up, dealing with family dynamics, family injustice, school-teacher pressure, disappointment and discrimination. I was delighted with their maturing view points and observations around family and parental comparisons. Developing insight and questioning was welcomed and celebrated as they developed empathy for others and realised they had a voice. Compared to others they were okay; others appeared privileged but that wasn't necessarily beneficial or an advantage. School life fluctuated with a revolving door of teaching styles and personalities, injustice and oppression mixed with power dynamics and games of strategy to orientate system and care-giver dominion.

People in authority over children can influence, guide and drive kids to be saints or sinners. If the child has harmful caregivers and negative teachers, that's double jeopardy. The children who orientate these two thorny pathways through their formative years are more likely to be deficit damaged as they head into their adulthood, and will view all their interactions with humans from a skewed blueprint based on multiple injustices. That's just a result from mild damage — it's far worse if the child has endured intense toxicity from parents, siblings, teachers, systemic failure and peer abuse.

Children suffer at different times in their formative years. If they have to cope with multiple challenges, unfair judgements, upheaval, unbalanced parents, poverty, abandonment, addiction or abuse they are in a perpetual cycle of viewing and forming their interpersonal relationships through the skewed lenses of confusion, emotional and physical pain, and silence. They are vulnerable to the culture and family norms that hold them bonded until their mid-teens. For some this is a wonderful developmental journey; others are incarcerated in a life of home and school unpredictability, mostly damage compounding on damage. Often this injurious experience has developed through multiple generations of family programming.

Falling through the cracks is so subtle for a kid. Hiding their pain, the child develops coping strategies, justifications and self-blames. From the beginning of this downhill spiral the kid starts to form a protective shell around themselves to shield themselves from further harm, insult, shame, confusion, multiple abuse, and neglect of their psychological, spiritual, physical and social needs.

Every adult has wounds of various degrees stemming from childhood hurts, but the scales of pain and injustice vary for all of us. A child exposed to multiple abuses over short periods can't process all this logically so creates a buffer that reflects out as a hard-to-penetrate defence system, just as a country develops a defence force to protect its borders. The difference is that some kids are like the USA, with a good democracy and an amazing defence system, and other kids are like Israel — always having to defend against frequent persecution.

Both countries have great defence systems, but only Israel has to regularly use theirs and this reflects in how its people view new people; they are constantly on edge waiting for attack. The psyche is pre-wired not to TRUST because of HISTORIC ABUSE…

Children enter their adolescence and mature into adults with all this programming based on their personal experiences and reactions thus far. Some are crippled by what they have endured getting to adulthood.

However some are strengthened by these same unjust circumstances, abuses and neglect. The difference could be hope, faith, resilience, or an amazing key person or circumstance that gave them support or perspective; helping them recognise their personal strengths to secure a strong foothold on life.

Foundations are what a person builds their future on. Regardless of whether they are thought about and reconfigured or not, the future will happen but a change of practice and belief can change the trajectory of experience and the future you end up with. Individual stories play forward into adult years, retirement years, family making, work choices, lifestyle habits, social interactions etc.

Speed Bump Personal Story Template

Your Age at Time of Event	Your Memory Recall	Your Reaction Behaviour	Your Feelings at the Time	Your Feelings Now
Pre-birth to 5 years old				
5 years old to 10 years old				
10 years old to 15 years old				
15 years old to 20 years old				
20 years old to 30 years old				
30 years old to 40 years old				
40 years onwards				

Figure 2

By unpacking your foundational programme you've chosen to become knowledgeable in the componentry of yourself.

Speed Bumps

Our yesterdays delivered speed bumps on our journey of growing towards this day. How successfully we orientated these bumps of pain and confusion depended on the resources made available at the time. As you progress through this composition it may be that some histories pop up to the surface, wanting a new resolution because you are reading a fresh resource.

For this purpose there is the **Speed Bump Personal Story Template** to record and timeline memories and feelings on.
(Figure on previous page)

Activity:

Copy this template into your notebook, making the columns and the timeline chronicling your age more workable for you. For example, if you are thirty years old, you won't need to add the extra years that are demonstrated on the template. This is your personal template so make it fit your age. When you read through the coming content and are triggered to document a memory, make it brief — just bullet-point facts, emotions, feelings. Don't feel you need to fill each section in — empty space is okay. This is about you so keep other people who were involved in the memory out of the content as much as you can. Remember the purpose is 'you can only change you not them'. Towards the end of this book you may have a smattering of feelings listed in the last column — *Your Feelings Now.* This is the area of work you need to clean up; the memory event was in the past yet you still have unresolved emotions and feelings that push and pull at how you live in the **present now** of your life.

The Beginning Foundation

In my personal journey I discovered that my intrinsic birth preamble was in fact my demise. I began life on the back foot, perpetuated by apathy, neglect, ignorance and mostly lack of research knowledge.

The era I was born in dictated thinking that the baby has simple needs: food, warmth, shelter basic cares — and lacks the cognition to understand its environment.

Today we have bodies of research that inform us a baby is being programmed while in utero. The baby hears environmental sounds, feels the emotions of the biological mother, and is harmed by substances taken by her.

It is feasible to view the beginning of your life as the platform where you start to interact, trust and establish relationships. These learned patterns carry you forward through-out life, and are added to by numerous experiences along the way. All these experiences influence and define how a person makes sense of subsequent interactions and observations.

This barrage of cues provides a mixed bag of influences — silent and verbal language, body language, family and cultural influence, and socio economic variance. They contribute to your personal projection and mannerisms, and define how you react or act with the wider group of humans sharing space with you.

This said, children who have experienced abuse and neglect anywhere from pre-birth forward into their formative years may have a different platform to assess trust and safety from. Any deficit may trigger the beginning of an imbalance in how they interact with the world. They have missed out on the secure childhood that teaches them how to be part of their world, how to be safe in it, how to trust in it, and how to identify who are the teachers of life programmes. If they are neglecting you, hating on you, are inconvenienced by you, struggling with you or feeling trapped by you this may well be caused by their lack of life skills.

When the beginning of your life is fucked up you have *no choice* but to be trained in your humanity from an imbalanced foundation. This reflects in limited attachments to others, and stunted self-esteem. Most childhood victims will ponder: Is it me who creates this stuff that makes me feel bad? Very few individuals recognise that it is others who create this pain, low self-worth, lacking trust, fear, damage, and the resultant skewed projection. Their initial mould is holding them in deficit.

Thankfully many children are born loved and are then celebrated, nurtured, socialised and cared for. However any onset of trauma or abuse later in life can still trigger an imbalanced platform of fear, phobia, hypervigilance, or lack of perspective. This change can skew interpersonal perspectives and behaviour as the victim develops new survival skills to orientate the traumatic or hidden memory. Thus these patterns are born and become the sorting board of their experience. The individual damage is further compounded if there has been very little intervention between the various bouts of abusive behaviour.

There are always survivors, an anomaly of personal strength and resilience, usually based in faith, hope, or from someone who helps them gather their natural resources and utilise them to cope and gain perspective. In my case I had an uncle who lived with us for a short while. He took me aside one day and said that my life was not right, that my mother was wrong, and that other families were different. This gave me perspective and helped me understand my observations.

When you look at the totality of life lived, childhood is phenomenal in gearing and steering you towards being a contributing adult. There should be a time of reflection on the values, beliefs and behaviours that govern your thinking thus far, and when you question them. Are they yours? Do they still honour who you are? Is this the person you want to be? Do you fit or belong, and if not why not? Are you authentically you or are you fearful of change? Who do you respect as a close adult and why?

In our fast-paced world there is *no time* made available for reflection, for redefining personal inner balance and for thinking. With a young adult everything is about the future plan, plus the fear of 'not enough' and 'not good enough'. They are governed by the pressure of high school grades, making a career choice and finding a life partner, and success in the eyes of peers, parents and society is measured by these. Adults still fall victim to this thinking in lesser degrees…

Running

I suggest you stop and think about your personal WELLNESS. Are you well? You have been running to achieve for years now, so are you tired? Are you sad? Are you dependent on escapism in drugs, sex, alcohol, gaming, people or sports? What's your hook? Are you at peace within yourself? Who are you? Can you form relationships, can you hold friendships, can you be alone, can you remove yourself from all devices, internet, phones, TV, magazines? Can you say 'I love you'? Can you hug and touch people? Can you be comfortable with someone hugging you? Are you comfortable without human touch? Do you want people to see you're not okay, or do you think that makes you weak? Is your vulnerability hidden from the world and from yourself, and if so where did this stem from? Do you remember these hurts, this pain that created your thoughts and behaviours? Do you want to change your programme now or at least be aware of it? Remember it's your default button producing behaviours that were possibly learned when you were a child. They got you to here, but are they the blueprint you want for your future? Are they the blueprint you want to influence your children with?

Now is your time to redefine your thinking, your patterns, your choices, and your relationship with yourself. If you view yourself as a computer hard drive, it's time to dump the programmes that are out-dated and weighing you down. They are in conflict with new thinking. It's time to sift and sort your stuff to make yourself more efficient and emotionally strong, and to redefine who you are now.

Who Am I? — A Product of All the Previous Years

The question is do you feel there may be some relevance with points raised in the previous reading?

Is there buried memory you feel affects you in some innate way, or are you totally aware that your formative years blatantly harmed you?

Do you sometimes cover up stuff or make excuses for your or your family's behaviour?

Were you, or did you, or do you experience the negative connotations of: belittling, neglect, abuse, insignificance, invisibility, unlovability, humiliation, shame or inferiority?

Did you develop coping mechanisms and/or behaviours of: hiding, protecting, surrogate parenting, pleasing, sacrificing, silence, aiding, aggression, acting out, reducing or blaming?

There are many reasons to explain personal behaviour and belief. Sadly, for some disarranged people their stories are camouflaged within exposure to toxic parenting, poor attachment, co-dependency, and quite possibly post-traumatic stress disorder (PTSD). Let's look at them now.

Toxic Parenting

Fuck off you little shit- I wish you were dead.

When we live in fear and confusion for all our early years or just a few months we are affected. This is trauma, whether subtle or in your face. It is perpetuated by lack of support, lack of knowledge, lack of understanding, and like most up bringings, takes place behind closed doors. Even when witnessed by caring adults, these behaviours are minimised because everyone likes to think the incidents are one-offs. Excuses are made that the carer is having a bad day; that kids are resilient, and will bounce back; that they caused the incident; or that they deserve the retribution.

Self-worth building is crafted from your birth and is enhanced and moulded by your lived experience of family love, support, and time invested in you. Self-worth is extended with wider family connections, friendship bonds, teaching and communities that support and encourage individuals as they grow into adulthood.

At any time you can grow positively or remain flat-lined, or be annihilated, and quite often all of this can be experienced by kids in one day. How they handle it is moving up and down a self-worth barometer... We can hope that over every week of their upbringing they are in the positive above 65% of the time.

Life has knocks for everyone. Some people experience more positives than negatives, while others experience more negatives than positives, and some just get a constant barrage of abuse from toxic parenting.

There are many cases where great parenting has produced kids who have gone off the rails, and many successful children who have endured terrible early lives yet have become stable, content, balanced adults. The *resilience* barometer is individual to everyone. What are the individual motivators that help one child orientate a safe passage through life emerging less damaged than a sibling who experienced the same harm? It could be age, independence, personal autonomy, support networks, inclusiveness or faith, to name but a few.

Toxicity is poisonous, but its effects vary from human to human.

Hypervigilance is one coping mechanism used by the child of toxic parenting — a fight/flight response of hypervigilant awareness to manage experiences. Some individuals will not have received emotional stability from parents. Therefore retreat, fear, anger, inappropriate behaviour, acting out, shrinking away and over-achieving are possible variations in these individual's responses as they try to manage their learned faulty programming.

Co-dependency, Care and Control

Fitting within a family group requires so many skills around roles, boundaries, performance, place value, income, status, rules, addictions, insecurity, interpersonal skills, confidence, escapism, self-regulation, bullying, antagonism, ridicule, relentless taunting, degradation, humiliation and plain unexplainable crazy behaviour.

It's like making a fruit smoothie — sometimes there are chunky things in the mix or the colours aren't appealing, or it smells funky, but it's all fruit and life-giving and if you're starving you swallow it down because we are human and have a predisposition to survive. Our mortality is the motivator.

How we all fit together in our family groups teaches us many skills. It also creates co-dependency traits for survival that serve while in the dependent family nest, but can become out-dated if not identified, and have lifelong, compounding effects on some or all of your relationships. They can even affect how you choose to parent your own children. This area needs exploration since co-dependency can cripple you in your adult years, and make you crumble into a damaged child every time you have to talk with or visit family at Christmas, birthdays, weddings, funerals or barbecues.

Can you feel the anxiety creep up your spine? The truth is that most families have things they hide — alcoholism, violence, prescription medications, bulimia, paedophilia, crime, exploitation, bribery, and financial manipulation or reward, so families develop a unified tolerance for this stuff. Co-dependency is when there is obsessive need of one person to control another person's behaviour. (Google search for a deeper explanation).

Co-dependency also happens within friendships and professional relationships, but for the purpose of this writing I emphasise family systems. Knowledge is power and it's important to be aware of why a significant family member can control your feelings by a look or gesture, and makes you question yourself for hours, days, years, or even beyond death. This may explain the inner battle or outward aggression you feel with intimate family members.

This area is massive and I do all the bodies of research no justice with a brief definition. If family events trigger any anger, confusion, guilt, stiffness, trapped feelings, self-harm, detached emotions, self-medication, comfort in eating, anger or depression, maybe you could seek clarity by reading about co-dependency. See how it fits with your personal confusions, fear of intimacy, fear of being hurt, fear of repeating the same old damaging patterns that lead to relationship disaster, financial hardship, alcoholism, or drug use, to name a few ways co-dependency can act out.

My own memory of co-dependent exposure in my family was my mother's fixation on drama, transforming minor events into crises involving the whole family. If you didn't buy into and become emotionally invested then you were alienated and ridiculed because you were selfish. My observation of my mother was that she created dramas just to feel alive.

All of these behaviours are distractions from your self-worth. They could stem from an outmoded blueprint based in fear and hurt caused intentionally, or inadvertently by your childhood and teenage years while growing up within the confines of the family unit…and could still be affecting the way you manage issues today.

At this point you should be identifying your insecurities, your interactions with others (friendships, work colleagues, in-laws, past lovers). Can you see a pattern or identify with the content thus far?

We initially are the sum of our upbringing and experiences, and are affected to some degree if left unchecked. Some of us are held frozen, stuck, trapped — a prisoner to our past that plays into our future.

Post-Traumatic Stress Disorder (PTSD)

The car crash that you survive at five is forgotten, but the attention deficit label you get later in your schooling is medicated; no one makes the link back to the trauma from the accident.

Most people are blind to Post Traumatic Stress Disorder (PTSD) and the impacts it can have when the trauma is not dealt with at the time through holistic, professional, respectful intervention.

The compounding effects of trauma are paralysing for groups and individuals when minimised, disregarded or ridiculed by themselves or others.

We live in a society where we are told to 'harden up' or 'suck it up' or 'move on' or 'that's the past' or 'build a bridge and get over it'. The truth is people mostly don't care or are not knowledgeable on what constitutes trauma or how to find help. They treat severe trauma the same way they support you with a cut knee — put a plaster on it and let time be the healer.

But not all wounds are the same. Some are invisible, and it's hard to put a plaster on when there's no obvious sign of injury.

With this topic, the focus is to educate you about your invisible wounds and the wounds of others, factoring in historical, present and future incidents. If you take anything from this work, please learn that you may be your own saviour or someone else's just by choosing to not reduce a traumatic experience, by remembering and honouring a traumatic memory and seeking specific help.

Every person is exposed to trauma. It can be a car accident, a sexual assault, abduction, a burglary, a home invasion, a beating, a betrayal, getting lost in a mall as a child, witnessing and participating in acts of war, witnessing murder, having an alcoholic parent.

Living through trauma exposure by being in it, amongst it or witnessing it can have long term effects for some individuals. Surprisingly, not everyone who shares the trauma experience will be affected the same way, and some not at all. This is where individual perception and resilience varies, with each person developing a unique coping and processing rationale.

Trauma imposes terrible violation on your reasoning capabilities. It sneaks into our too-hard basket and sometimes hides under the carpet. It's the elephant in the room that we simply have to camouflage, deny. It's an assault on our sensory control mechanism. It's horrible and violating and confusing. It is not rational, it is not kind and it steals your soul. It is too big to fathom so we adapt and hide it. Leading trauma expert Bessell Van Der Kolk identifies that the emotions and physical sensations of trauma imprints are not stored as memories but come to the fore as disruptive physical reactions in the present life of the person.

PTSD is now recognised widely among the medical community. It is highly recognisable in the case of dramatic trauma exposure, but easily overlooked in cases of hidden trauma memory or minimised trauma inflicted by key people, or where the individual disassociated at the time of trauma.

It is our job to raise awareness of PTSD behaviours. These could include self-harming, or terrors displayed in behaviour patterns that have no reasoning or memory to the trauma experience. PTSD can cause changes in behaviour that restrict the authentic autonomous self from being content without fear or worry. It can present in avoidance, or living in a mind fog. Our knowledge can help individuals connect their personal dots, or the reader may identify this as a possibility in asking the right questions of themselves or others about trauma exposure...   Take a moment to breathe...

Now... Consider How You Attached

When life throws us lemons we dodge them, we suck them and at times we wade in lemon juice, but for some individuals they have only known how to swim in lemon juice. Constant bathing in the juice would have an uncomfortable effect on an individual's skin over time; maybe eczema develops in the cracks, then irritation, bleeding, and unsightly rashes.

Your focus is on coping with the discomfort, not realising the cause is the lemon juice. You spend your time distracted with managing your sores while trying to fit with the clear-skinned people and hoping they don't see your imperfection. You have honed strategies of hiding your skin condition under layers of clothing, and when occasionally someone notices you have an excuse ready.

Wouldn't life be easier if you knew that you were at a disadvantage by bathing in lemon juice? That others were bathed in water because their carers knew that lemon juice would strip the PH balance of their skin, causing damage?

This analogy leads into impacts of poor attachment to your birth parents, or the lack of consistent care with a significant loving, caring, nurturing and attentive carer. In the absence of a family you can survive but to thrive you must know love, nurture, trust and safe physical touch, as well as respectful, honest, sensitive communication.

For me, this is where my foundation was out of balance — all during my formative development I bathed in lemon juice.

Attachment theory is the explanatory model drawn from psychology. This identifies that infants are at risk of not developing the right building blocks in their brain if they have minimal or no opportunity to form an attachment to a caregiver in the first few years of life. It is further jeopardised with ongoing emotional and physical neglect and abuse.

We need to be aware of the ongoing effects on infants of the physical or emotional absence of their parents or primary caregivers. These absences can scramble the inner organisation of the infant's brain, and damage future interactions with primary caregivers, friendship bonds, and learning as life goes on. This absence of quality care leads the child to difficulty with forming trust in friendship and relationship throughout childhood.

Quality care enables an infant to develop secure attachment to a responsive, invested carer or parent. The toddler develops trust in the caregiver, and recognises sensory and emotional cues. The toddler mirrors the actions and emotions of the care.

When I was nine months old I found a home. I was the third child to fit into the family. I thank them for saving me from an unknown future and for giving me love, security, and moral fortitude.

I was adopted in an era when the belief was that a baby is too young to remember. Babies might not verbally recall early memory but we all know intrinsically when we are abandoned. It sticks to the fibre of our cellular memory and hurts anew with any further abandonment throughout life. It shows up in behaviours such as breaking up friendship and intimate relationships. We are already hypersensitive to being not good enough, so we suck our hurt in and walk back into that hard shell of protection that was formed early in our life to buffer the confusing assault of our inner processing mechanism.

The healing comes with understanding that your programme has glitches and that you need to reboot your inner child with knowledge, fun, and love. My healer was having the opportunity to parent four amazing kids. Along with the parenting that I invested in them I was conscious that I was re-parenting myself. The love and pleasure exchanged in this bonding was being experienced by me as an adult as first experiences, filling in the missing cognitive building blocks of my first year of life.

The way I realised I was healing my inner child is beautiful. As I said I have four kids, and when each child reached ten months old I would instinctively remember all of these months, time, love, care, concern, joy, celebration, attention and firsts: teeth, words, smiles, steps, crawling and standing. I was never actively conscious of the ten-month marker approaching; it would just be an overwhelming realisation that would arrive for a day, and I would think, *Wow, that's what I missed out on.* After my fourth baby generated this cathartic experience I realised that regardless of how many babies I birthed and nurtured, my memory of the loss of parenting would be held in me forever.

How You Fit to Your Foundation

This section introduced types of behavioural or psychological exposure that can negatively impact a person, yet sometimes create personal strengths. The writing only touched on what harm, hurt and strength look like. You may well be thinking and reflecting on your own early life exposure, or thinking of someone you know who might have been exposed to some of the wrongs mentioned. The content is thought provoking, shocking, and truly educating about finding your footing, locating your place value in your life thus far, and realising you can knowledgably recreate foundational belief moving forward.

Breathe deeply and release the breath slowly several times. You have now followed new knowledge, processed it and tried to identify with it. Congratulations. If the content has been hard to absorb, then take your time since the next part of this writing will tackle your personal evaluation of where you fit with your early life foundation and how you get to reframe and move forward through it, embracing your personal power and connecting with your personal autonomy. The purpose of this work is self-empowerment — maybe for you, or maybe for someone you know.

Having an understanding of the first foundation of your life is powerful in a change or healing process. Even if part of your foundation is dodgy or crap — or all of it — then thankfully you can change the next foundation you lay down without unknowingly carrying over thoughts, behaviours or useless harming patterns that trip you up or cripple you with your adult journey through life.

We as humans constantly measure ourselves against others whether it be: financial, body image, attractiveness, clothing style, media devices, music choice, skin colour, education, sporting ability, assets, suburbs, career choice, friends — the list goes on. I think we spend so much time gazing at the surface and hardly ever viewing the foundation.

If a person is a house we see their style, we gaze in the windows and see the wall colourings and furnishings. Some people become judgemental, envious, or wishful. Nobody wonders about their foundation, yet a good foundation will hold a house up throughout life's challenges.

When you look at family, friends, peers and celebrities you are subliminally comparing yourself to other people's foundations that you can't see and even they often can't see for themselves. Assessing your own foundation is where you can take charge of your own direction moving forward. This is the burning ground of all the shitty experiences you didn't order for yourself.

In essence, if you assess your foundation you can liberate yourself from parts of your story that don't have any merit in your future contentment.

Understanding your history will be an individual process — scary and black, fun and weird. You are not alone; we all have pivotal moments, and black holes of confusion. It takes courage to freefall to the bottom of the pain pit of conscious or repressed memories, reacquainting yourself with memories of how you fit in your world.

As you unpack things like fear, limitation, depressive episodes, anxiety, shame, judgement — as well as hope, motivation, personal power and strength — you get to make choices about what you value, and what gets deleted.

Section Two - Part 1

Finding Our Place

Question Your Worldview

Don't be satisfied with stories. How things have gone with others. Unfold your own myth.

Rumi.

Every person has a worldview as does every society, and this framework of ideas, values, belief, bias, and attitudes influences how individuals and groups live in the world. A worldview is formed from the influences of family, ethnicity, culture and community norms and values that mould an individual. It is said to be a mental model of reality pertaining to how an individual and society interpret things, thus becoming an individual and cultural concept that may view reality either negatively or positively.

One concept of *Locate Yourself* is to understand how the first foundation and worldview work together. By reassessing first beliefs in the light of new knowledge the individual has a formula to change their thinking and situation. I believe that any disarranged person has the potential to become a rearranged person with new knowledge, and this is the fundamental purpose and plan of *Locate Yourself*.

The aim of section two is for you to locate yourself within your understanding of your worldview. Think about your beginnings and your current views on these coming topics, and intentionally extend your knowledge to access where these thoughts came from. Question yourself: do they honour you now, or is it time to rethink aspects of the formula that defines your belief system?

With knowledge you can decide if you want to be a chocolate cake, a light marble cake, a rich mud cake or that flamboyant rainbow cake. A person can bake any cake if they have the ingredients and a recipe. The recipe for the cake is known to the cook; maybe the cook can bake only chocolate cake because they are the only ingredients they are aware of. The cook knows there are many types of cake but is limited to the ingredients of his/her foundation, worldview concepts, and assimilated learning thus far.

At this point realise that worldview is fluid. It changes when an individual changes their belief with new knowledge. Individual change can go on to create community and culture change — therefore creating social change for groups within societies. An example of worldview change has been the global acceptance of civil union and same gender-marriage at a legislative level in the last decade. Whereas thirty years earlier people were marginalised, excluded, prosecuted and medically treated for mental health disorders if they were attracted to people of the same gender.

Section two is a thought-provoking journey into beliefs, experiences and observations. This section introduces several topics not necessarily connected logically or sequenced. Each topic is a musing to locate yourself within your experiences of wider systems that help and hinder our interpretation of the world. These systems help define our attitudes, opinions, beliefs, and to some extent our behaviours.

Systems add Structure

Locate Yourself is about you on all levels, but we are never just us. We belong to groups, and we fit and float across systems. Mostly we have free will about our level of involvement within these systems, but there are systems that have a dominant discourse. These systems hold us fairly as long as we are compliant to their rules of function.

That said we live in a democracy that needs structure, compliance, reliability, governance and enforcement, hence the need to have systems. Some systems pertinent to an individual quality of life are: economic systems, education systems, food systems, health systems, family systems, legal systems, culture systems.

Urie Bronfenbrener's Socio-Ecological Framework and Process-Person-Context-Time model (PPCT) (below) shows how an individual is surrounded by systems through their life course. For the purpose of this guide the information presented on Bronfenbrener's evolving socio-ecological model is a simplistic explanation. A Google search will provide more detailed information for readers who require deeper understanding of this theory.

Bronfenbrenner's Bioecological Model of Human Development.

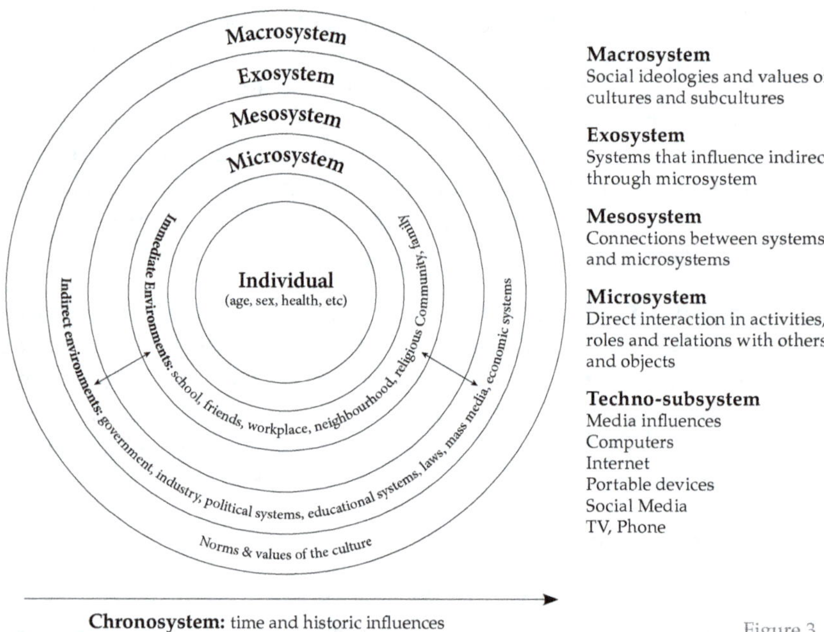

Figure 3

If you take some time to study the above model it should connect the dots of the topics being discussed within section two's reading. *Locate Yourself* is about the *Individual* person understanding their place within these systems, and the symbiotic influence transferred across them. Social ecology is about the social, institutional and cultural context of people and their relationship with their environment.

Predominantly in section three there is encouragement to locate your tribe. Before you can do that, section two now asks you to understand the interface of human development and the immediate systems of influence that have imposed views, rules, social conditioning and cultural norms on you, and ultimately how these have contributed to the formation of your self-belief and wider beliefs, attitudes, opinions and behaviour.

The point being that as you move forward you get to unpack your thinking around your past influences.

Personal Autonomy

Unpacking your past is a choice to drive your thinking in a curious and empowering direction. It can be liberating or a scary negotiation, like decluttering your bedroom — choosing what to keep, what is useful, what is comforting.

The backbone of this writing raises awareness that we don't all come from similar backgrounds or equality. Personal autonomy once achieved is the realisation that you are a free-thinking individual who has opinions derived from your own thinking and reflective processing. Such a person has an awareness of their independence from significant others opinions and decisions over or about them. I believe autonomy is when you can distinguish 'where do they end and I begin'. It is when you start to speak and plan for yourself.

Personal autonomy is governed by your world view, and as we know this is guided by the micro, meso, and macro systems (Bioecological Model Pg 29), being, your childhood, school systems, family systems, faith systems, peers and neighbourhood, political thought, deprivation, economics, race, gender, culture, health and media. Each individual is subliminally storing prejudice and opinion from influences surrounding them. The child and young person morph into these beliefs because they are experiencing active dependence; their beliefs are defined by all the influences bombarding them daily.

Coming out the other side of adolescence is an arduous journey for most people. Everything is open for challenge. This is the time to speak for yourself, and migrate into your individuality. It's also a challenging time of re-evaluation of where do your thoughts, opinions and biases come from, who influenced you, and do you agree with your inherited belief system?

The earlier mentioned decluttering of the bedroom analogy comes into play here. It's the burning ground of the groupthink of family systems, peer group influences, behaviour and beliefs that don't fit with an individual now. This is a fantastic time to evolve, redefine and extend personal view. It is important to mention that we are connecting individual development and microsystem dots now.

Personal autonomy development typically happens in the teenage years, but depending on cultural mores, cognitive function, personality, circumstances, health and aging it can develop and disappear at any stage. Change can be threatening; as you open your mind and heart up to choosing to explore your preconceived assumptions from a new mindset, you may encounter debate, ridicule and persecution from those around you.

Change Maker

Personal autonomy is the change maker in your humanness. Your beliefs are what you mirror out to the world. But collecting several varied aspects around one belief is the humanity that effects change and breaks down barriers. This is where the individual influences the micro and meso groups (refer to the ecological model).

People often self-question with inner thoughts about things that need change. There will be others who have wondered about the same issue and just didn't know how to voice their thoughts. Change comes about by physical effort, verbal effort, or email effort.

Realising you are alone in the change process can be daunting. Very few people want to change because it's hard, and many people find security in familiarity. Personal change is just that — personal change, as in you evolving. You are geared to be a change maker; you have the tenacity to question, the vision, and a focus on handing on a better legacy to your children. But this will involve challenging people to rethink the legacy they were left.

Change makers are deemed radical and different in family systems and society. Defining yourself as a questioner of values, morals, language and behaviour can make you the antagonist in groupthink. My advice is to save your energy after a couple of attempts. Move your thoughts to changing yourself, not them. Model your newness. If the language of your family or friends group is demeaning, use better words. If your family or friends choose to use substances, make yourself absent so you are not pressured to partake. If your family or friends are violent remove yourself, get safe, and tell someone who has the power to help. In the short term the people you confront won't like your viewpoint, but you might just start to like yourself.

- In life the bravest thing you'll ever do is set yourself free.

- Change yourself, not them.

- Take your power back.

- Have courageous conversations with others and key professionals.

- Move through the stages of victim, survivor, and liberator.

As a free-thinking family member and valued part of society you have the right to question anything. It is also your right to advocate for change. If you see or experience cruelty in your family or friends group or wider community, talk about it. Recognising the cycle and trying to break it takes huge courage. Making change is often dangerous with family because they don't like change. Before you tackle family dysfunction be prepared for an angry backlash. Make sure you have support systems in place — friends, partner, counsellor, someone who has your back — so you can debrief the details and find wisdom, guidance, confidentiality and emotional support.

There are many disenfranchised family members living estranged from each other because of such confrontations. Never lose sight of a successful outcome from a family challenge. Change can happen quickly or not at all. Be prepared for the status quo to remain unchanged. When you raise awareness around issues that need exploration you become an advocate for yourself and others. This role, once initiated, will never be forgotten and will become easier as you tackle future injustices.

Coercive Power

It may sound harsh but sometimes you have to be ruthless to protect yourself from other people's behaviours. And sometimes people may have to fear your domination.

Coercive power and power over is when someone or something has power over you, or you hold power over people or things. Coercive power can be an authority figure, sibling, friend or parent who has power to reward or take things away. Examples of this can be employers and school systems since you have to abide by their rules. Parents use power over when they threaten withdrawal of affection or things if the child challenges them, or behaves in a way that conflicts with the parent's thinking.

In relating back to the ecological model, we are focusing on the *individual* who has direct interaction with the immediate environments of school, family, work, friends and neighbourhood within the *microsystem*. The *individual* also interacts with the *techno-subsystem* which has no boundary. The mutual sharing of language, geography, and to a point interests should see similarity with values and rules through the connections across the *microsystem, mesosystem and techno-subsystem*. There is a grey area across all the power sharing-systems with structural rules. Within the systems are personalities who use systems to feel powerful, to get their own needs met, and sometimes perversely to create drama.

Some personalities and organisations either knowingly or unwittingly use coercive power to control, separate, manipulate, blame, accuse, exploit, intimidate or frighten a person into submission. Intimidating behaviour — whether it be via social media, email, texting, verbal or physical attack, rumour, scapegoating, perversion, exclusion, isolation, trapping, detaining, pressurising, threatening, blackmail, grooming, and bullying — are good indicators that you are in a power struggle.

There is power over in most relationships to varying degrees, but people usually find a balance. Family systems are rife with the dynamic of power struggles. A baby holds all the power when it screams, and a toddler when it twists and contorts in the supermarket carpark while onlookers judge your parenting ability. These are usually short-time-frame power struggles. Long-term power struggles are harming, and the only way to find safe ground is to remove yourself from the game. By doing this you have personal space to think, and to analyse why you feel on edge around this person or these people.

My story I choose to share is a lesson I learnt from my mother. First I want to emphasise she parented mostly well and was known as having a big heart, but she sometimes couldn't get past her need to have power over and of course she loved creating drama and involving people in it. My mother died a few years back and I have never experienced so much grief at her loss; she left me longing for her words just one more time. I truly loved that big woman with a big smile, a big heart and a big body to match. This is one of our stories that I put into the category of ignorant parenting. The words I use to describe the event came years later with my social-work studies. At the time of the event I was 21 years old and I had few words — just feelings of being in danger, and unsafe with my mother and her actions.

I had been living in my brother's house and was shifting out this day, but like all house shifts it took longer than expected. My brother thought I was being unreasonable; we had angry sibling words and I ended up throwing a small cardboard carton of milk at him. In turn he went and told my mother. My mother came over, we had a screaming match, and she instructed a friend of my brother to physically restrain me with my hands behind my back. I got a couple of punches in to him, but he was a black belt in martial arts, he restrained me effectively. At this point I'm verbally abusive, so my mother starts to slap my face repeatedly, telling me she would involve the police and have me committed to a mental health facility because she had witnesses. I was quick to ascertain how unsafe I was. I quietened my voice, they released the hold and I very quickly left the house, not to speak with her again for the next two and a half years. I removed myself from the family, disenfranchising myself for my own safety.

The reason I felt unsafe was because I had seen her commit someone earlier that year. My mother's background was nursing. It was very easy for her to commit a person since she knew the requirements. I knew she would use my brother and his friend as witnesses, and exaggerate the story. This is an example of coercive power and power abuse at its most intimate, and this is also domestic violence.

The loss of family for personal safety and autonomy was worth the sacrifice. I had one brother whom I felt safe with and he supported my decision. The irony is I then lived with an abusive boyfriend to get away from an abusive mother because he was the safer choice. I gained a lot of strength in myself and eventually left him. Then I restored a working relationship with my mother and the family members through embracing forgiveness. My mother was open to negotiation because of the community shame of having a disenfranchised daughter, and maybe she thought she had overreacted. We could never agree on where the injustice sat, so we agreed not to agree.

There are two healers that need to be expanded on: one is personal strength and the other is time. Both are incredibly powerful. Social work leans on identifying people's strengths and making them aware that they have personal resources to help them obtain and maintain their autonomous life. Earlier I said resilience leads to strength, which is true, but adversity also leads to developing strengths to cope with life changes. Growing your personal power is strength, as is using your intuition and understanding, trusting your feelings, gaining knowledge, asking for help, and using your voice to have courageous conversations. You would be surprised how many strengths you have acquired in your life.

Activity:

Identify your **strengths** and list them in your notebook to remind yourself about your personal power cupboard.

Time Rationale

Time became my friend and healer. I first embraced it with the previously mentioned two and a half years of self-directed separation from my mother and family. Time allowed me the processing space during that long sit away from my family dynamics.

In my late twenties I would have to attend family functions. Some were good, but most had a weird vibe due to power and control dynamics between some extended family members. You never knew until you got there what the vibe would be. I started to become anxious with the anticipation of these events, and then wasted more time worrying about the kind of negative wall I would be greeted with. I then realised I was investing more time in worrying before the event than the invested time at the function. The maths didn't add up. That's when I created my time rationale. I would go to every event with a 'worst case' plan of give it two hours — go late and leave early. I sometimes utilised it, but mostly I found joy among the group.

This time limited / time invested strategy has worked several times in my life. Taking power back on how you invest your time is strength. Time is something that we all have, but we need to understand its importance to living and how to reduce our stress associated with the way time can pressurise us as individuals.

Eckhart Tolle in his famous book *The Power of Now* is the guru of understanding time. He breaks time down into psychological time — which is the identification with the past — and compulsive projection into the future, hence precoding future events. He says to live in the present moment; make short visits to past memory and future desire.

I tell you, this man is poetry. When things are getting hectic in my life and I'm starting to race ahead I pull back on Eckhart's words and remind myself I only have now so how do I want to use it wisely? This centres me and the magic of balance becomes my calm again.

We are programmed from all our influences about time. Everything is measured by it, and we are taught that there is not enough, or death is coming and time is running out. Time is reduced to a limitation, yet when I enter a meditative state I'm in a state of no mind, or stillness, and fully present at the same time. I use this to gain management of my own time, because I am relaxing and rebalancing my energy to become effective in my use of analogue time. So I use meditation to gain time.

Time can be unbearable when you are in the grip of something horrible. At this point you can't master time. You may only cope with increments of one day, or one hour or one minute or one breath. If you are in crisis or addiction this is the reality of immediate time, and it is impossible to bring a time focus in as a healing antidote. We all know things pass but please don't patronise someone's trauma with sayings like 'it will pass in time' or 'time is a healer', since this could be more harmful than helpful in the moment.

People rush time positively when they are anticipating an exciting event, like a baby being born, or a wedding, or a coming visit from a dear friend. People can also dread time when anticipating a visit from a family member, or a wedding, or the birth of a child. Both situations emanate energy, like being caught up in drama. I think you need to own your understanding of how you work with time; it could be that you disrespect time more by dreading an event or focusing too much on the restrictions time delivers you, thus making you lose your personal power over increments of analogue time.

Nelson Mandela was incarcerated for around 27 years in a cell; he used time effectively, working in a meditative state to find and hold his personal power. You would think this was a waste of time, but he mastered time, and in his peace he transpired that to his fellow prisoners, his prison guards and his visitors. That message was fed back to the international community to aid his release, with the human cry to end apartheid in South Africa. All Nelson was afforded was time in prison and the mental freedom of how to live within that time.

Culture

> *Behave towards everyone as if receiving a quest.*

Chinese Proverb.

When we travel we become exposed to different ethnicities and cultures which present as exotic to our own culture. We embrace this difference because we are the travellers; we want that cultural exchange and diversity. We are curious and respectful because we are extending our awareness by observing difference. We are in control of our opinions about what we like and don't like about the affront of difference. We are tourists in another culture.

Oddly, we are more embracing of learning another culture when we travel than when we work and live in communities of difference and rich diversity. First the tourist is paying to see difference — they have financial power. They expect to mix with difference across all their senses but they are in control of the choice and level of exotic exposure — it doesn't occur in their space. Yet at home in their suburb they may be threatened on a subliminal level by difference; their thoughts and/or actions may be intentionally or ignorantly racist. This ignorance or reaction can create secular communities of people closing the door of welcome to new people entering their world.

Culture is in all of us; we all stem from ethnicities that connect us to people, music, dance, ritual, flavour, creation stories, faith and diversity. Bronfenbrenner's *ecological model* has culture in the outermost ring of the *macrosystem,* forming the umbrella that our values, ideologies, rituals, arts, communication, language, governance and systems are impressioned and defined from. These are fluid, like our worldview, due to how time *(chronosystem)* and social change can alter culture both negatively and positively, forming histories. We live in geographical regions *(exosystems)* that group us to cultural judgements and inclusions. These areas *(microsystems)* reorganise us into types of people: socio-economic status, ethnicities, prejudice and opportunity. We attend churches, clubs and organisations, which further narrow the groupings to cultural norms. Lastly we are narrowed and defined by our family group culture. Inside all of this is the *individual I am.* You have so many connections.

As you can see, we are the sum of many influences from things outside us. Family groups are where we establish our first foundation and can be wonderful or not. Some people own their culture; they stand strong in their sense of identity and culture values, and they have pride that radiates out from their presence. Their cultural belonging and practices flow into their biological, psychological, social and spiritual aspects of themselves.

I, on the other hand, felt like an imposter clinging on the edge of other cultures while I tried to define mine. My foundation was skewed because of my adoption into a culture that didn't 'feel' right. I was always searching for my 'loving, understanding people'. This sounds weird but you know in your gut when you just don't feel complete.

Activity:

Think about the cultural influences that define you. Write them in your notebook.

- Ponder your cultural bias.

Realise that your culture grows when you grow.

Culture aligns every nuance of your life influences, both negatively and positively. An outsider looking in at you may view as negative what you define as positive. This could minimise their cultural influences that hold them strong. Every culture has their norms that form belonging, and belonging is the fundamental need of all human beings across all culture groups on this planet. Every culture has a perspective that needs respect. Every culture needs people to be inquisitive about their diversity, observing their own culture and that of their neighbours to find common ground — being tolerant of difference, and inclusive of understanding. We all come from nuances of difference and sameness; our values have a beginning and grow, change shape, and extend us, creating a rich tapestry of connections to humanity.

There are, however, cultural behaviours that can be abusive. The saying 'when in Rome, do as the Romans do' does not justify turning our back on abuse within a culture. This is called cultural relativism. In effect it is saying a behaviour that is deemed abusive by the cultural blueprint and legislation of your country will not be challenged by the same value standards of care and protection. You are extending your moral and legal boundaries when you allow an abusive cultural practice to be allowable because you think this is 'their way' of administering discipline, or of maintaining moral and health control.

Never be a bystander to abuse if you can safely intervene. If you can be the change maker by alerting the authorities then please step up and help.

School Life

You throw thorns, falling in my silence they become flowers.

Guatama Buddha.

Accumulated school experience and learning can affect a person's first foundation, and then continue to influence their worldview through their recount of school experience, teachers and career choices.

Education is the fundamental right of all children, though there is some leniency about how this education is administered. Most people attend big schools with lots of personalities. School can be a nightmare for some and an oasis for others.

Accessible education is a ticket out of despair for some — a currency for freedom in life. Education is a privilege for most of the world's children, and a meeting place for peer communities. Within the education system are school teachers and schools — some great, some average, and some under-delivering.

Within the *ecological model* the school is placed in the *microsystem*. The *individual* at the centre of the model has behavioural variability, but must fit the school environment which is linear in rules, objectives, disciplines, processes and purpose. The *microsystem* has family, friends, faith and neighbourhood communities surrounding the *individual.* School practice is heavily reliant on the *techno-subsystem* to gratify the need for instantaneous information sourcing. The *exosystem* holds the structural systems that are the policy holders and regulators of the education system, health system, legal system, economy and media. These influence the communities in the *microsystem*, which then flow into the *individual I AM.* The *individual I Am* can struggle or flourish inside the school environment.

School can be fun, extremely social and stimulating. Teachers can be inspirational and nurturing. There will always be salt and pepper memories of school years. Our memory will recall cool teachers, cruelty imposed by teachers, good schools, great schools and problem schools, and the times when things didn't make sense, or when it was the most dreaded environment that created internalised fear and anxiety. Our memories are based on the impacts of school on us.

What I want to emphasise is the trouble and confusion some children can bring from a cocktail of behaviour in their home life that is acted out at school. The memory for the child will then be associated with school; they rarely associate the memory with being an extension of and reaction to life at home. Educationists understand this process and schools try to provide counsellors and guidance. When a child is closed to this help from fear of family retribution, peer retribution or wider school shame, they struggle to open up to trust that an outside source will be able to help them.

Hopefully your education was flawless, or you had alternate years bouncing between good and poor school experiences. If you're outside these measures then school is damned hard work.

Children with learning challenges suffer their way through education; they struggle with the workload and with the learning comparison of class peers. The learning-challenged child is aware of their place within the tier of classroom assessments. This alone affects a child's foundation moving into an adult life. Self-worth is challenged and they can limit their own potential if left unsupported. They will develop strategies that will reduce exposure to their learning challenge, just as a child who struggles with swimming or is body conscious will choose to forget their swimsuit, so as not to expose their insecurity. These patterns of survival from humiliation will follow them forward and can limit their career pathways if left unchecked.

Learning and physical-challenge supports are in education institutions and are geared to help people get the help they need to succeed in a career direction. This in turn reflects on a better worldview of how education can be manipulated to meet the needs of a young person, or of an adult climbing a barrier to make a better go at education second time around.

Fortunately the world over has benefited from the internet. Personal devices give global 24/7 access to any type of learning, business, communication and gratification. Schools have diversified with the internet expansion, being able to target learning styles and offer ability-specific programmes to enhance individual learning, both within and outside the curriculum and school environment. The internet has also changed learning focus to a 'lifelong' learning trend with e-university options.

Instant Information

The transfer of information is phenomenal; we live in an instantaneous information system. When we look at the *ecological model*, we can see how the speed of information sharing is changing our culture. Culture is in the outermost layer of the *macrosystem*, feeding and defining the values and norms of a geographical region in the way it flavours itself. The internet is dominating the spread of trends, global news sharing, social media, and all manner of niche subculture dialogue and image. Does this mean that the individuality of global cultures are morphing into a dilute version of themselves, and are we at risk of trading unique flavour for fast-changing global nuance and trends? Change is good, but are you internet cautious? Or are you skipping along the information superhighway, gleefully blind to how fast you are travelling?

Traditionally in the *ecological model,* media belonged to the *exosystem,* which transferred across all the systems in either direction. The recent introduction of the *techno-subsystem* now dominates, uniting the world with information and social media, thereby bringing all manner of macro, exo, meso, and *microsystem* communities and individuals together. The internet is a global liberator for choice and speed of information, changing our worldview about the way things are done, interpreted, recorded, frenzied, archived and shared. People are choosing to live vicariously and voyeuristically in other people's stories, which can be inspiring and motivational. YouTube is a path that shortens the fame trail for many people, bringing variety and opportunity to share talent and/or weird stuff. It's also a medium that can allow the voiceless a voice, and make groups of widely separated (geographically speaking) individuals (eg. those with rare health conditions) come close together.

However, the internet is also an oppressor for some. Social media hurts people with cyber bullying, shaming, hate crimes, and unsolicited and uncensored terrorism. The victims of these abuses did not give their consent for the insensitive, voyeuristic shaming of their person.

Other victims of the internet and electronic devices are friends and family members. Society is so fixated with being online that they forget about the people in their immediate vicinity. Within the *microsystem* people are information gathering, sharing or stalking, even while they are present and supposedly socialising with others. Society is changing as people have a device attached to their person for all of their waking hours. 'Online-onbody' is a phenomenon that needs self-regulation and management. The victims are the people who want you to see them, hear them and be present with them when they need closeness. The other victim is the one absorbed in the device as they distance themselves from closeness.

Look to your foundation to remember when someone missed your emotional crises, failing to give you attention because they were absorbed in an electronic device.

The *individual* at the centre of the *ecological model* is experiencing confusion and hurt feelings when nobody sees their need for emotional support. Children experience emotional deficit when their caregivers/parent are primarily consumed with an electronic device, shifting quality focus and attention from the child.

In effect the child's value is reduced to being present, but not being seen. With perpetuated, repeated experience of this absent attention, a child's worldview is moulded to think that all love and attention is delivered staccato and shared with a screen.

Sigmund Freud (1923) identified three components to psyche/personality: the Id, Ego and Superego. The Iceberg Metaphor model (next page) is a structural representation to demonstrate Freud's theory regarding the components of human thought processes. It touches on the preconscious and unconscious areas where unresolved confusion, neglect, and trauma rest. (An expanded explanation is recommended with a Google search).

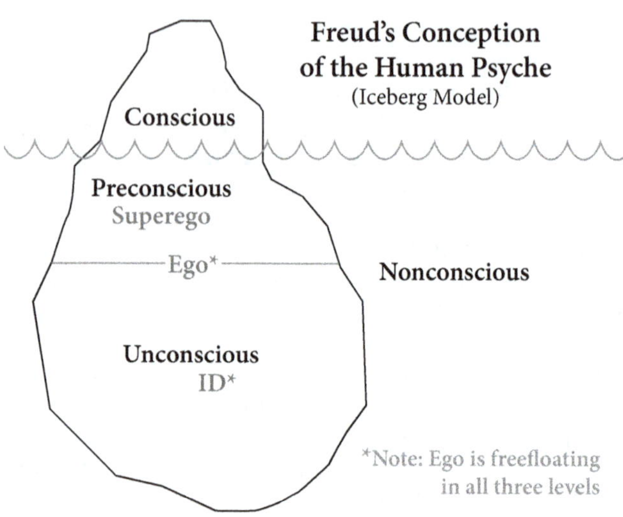

Figure 4

The Iceberg Model shows the tip of the iceberg above the waterline. This represents conscious reality (thinking and quick memory recall). Below the waterline is the Preconscious, which is the place of dreams and deeply stored memory. It also holds the Superego which is critical (self) analysis and moral regulation, and the Ego which regulates decision making and reasoning between the desires and pleasure need of the Id and the moral regulation of the Superego. Below that in the unconscious area is the Id, which drives instinctual desire and pleasure principle while responding to restraint by the Ego with reasoning. If that restraint fails because the pleasure seeking Id is very determined, the Superego steps in with moral and value control. The unconscious is where human thinking stores confusion, trauma and intuition.

Freud states that the Superego is the memory bank of the values and morals of society, and that you learn them from your parents, other people and your surroundings. The challenge for children experiencing device-deficit parenting is maintaining their personal value and reinforcing their personal self-worth with the ongoing emotional neglect and the damage of invisibility, due to having to share space and attention with caregivers who are absorbed with the distraction effects of internet technology. This is the legacy they model to their children, and set the tone for the next generation to also suffer the negative effect of being ignored.

The Id is pleasure seeking, and social media and the instantness of the internet feeds instant gratification. Thereby growing a stronger Id personality. This in turn could become the dominant driver of generations to come, changing the value fibre invested in raising children and holding friendship. Does this mean that social media becomes equal with face-to-face relationships?

The internet never stops. Technology is constantly evolving and humans want to morph into technology. Where does stillness and balance enter a person's lifestyle when they are constantly online — uploading, downloading, sharing, profile building and stalking? Self-regulation is required for attaining inner and outer balance.

Personal Needs

> *What is necessary to change a person is to change his awareness of himself.*
>
> Abraham Maslow.

Now I want to lead your thinking into identifying your personal needs to see if they are being met or if you can locate gaps that have caused hardship.

Deficiency around unmet needs can impact our belief and attitude towards those who we perceive to have 'more' than us. This is then reflected in our thoughts and behaviours towards opportunity, abundance, love, family values and self-esteem.

Maslow's Hierarchy of Needs Pyramid.

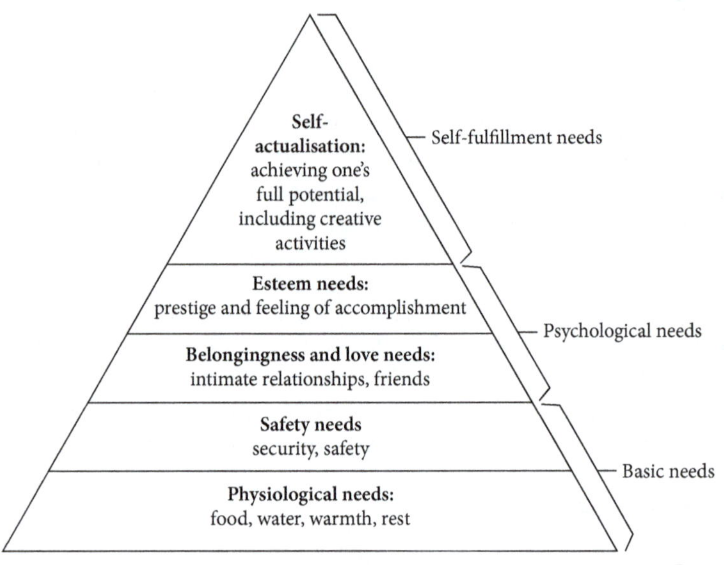

Figure 5

Abraham Maslow's 'hierarchy of needs' pyramid is the visual teaching model that will explain the process of locating and understanding met and unmet needs. The pyramid demonstrates that we need to meet our important needs before we run ahead and try to meet the needs we want most. So we need to first identify our important needs for surviving safely in our present life situation.

Obviously we need to feel secure, with somewhere to sleep at night — somewhere to call home. We need food and water to support our body. These are physiological survival needs. They are not necessarily clear-cut for everyone, because the home may not supply safety in the case of sexual abuse or domestic violence. Food can be life supporting, or not prioritised by your carers. These are the gaps that impact many families.

Another fundamental requirement is the need to belong with fellow humans. This could be with family, friends, social media networks, sport groups, school and church communities. How you *choose* to belong is individual, and most of us need to form attachments and trust with family or a significant person in our early life.

Now we will start to identify unmet needs. Unmet needs can be traumatic or subtle.

An example of subtle unmet needs is a young woman who shared her early life story with me. She was supporting her brother coming out of prison, and was hoping he would stay out longer this time. They were tight, their bond cemented in the upbringing of child abuse and neglect. He had been doing burglaries since he was very young, always stealing food and clothes for both of them. Their mother was a party girl; all of her social support benefit went into alcohol and drugs. This is what was constantly on the kitchen table every morning before they went to school — half-finished beer bottles, marijuana — and there was always a barrage of new people sleeping over. That's their memory of home life. The young woman felt responsible for her brother in his adult years because he had provided for her basic needs from early childhood.

Sadly this family story is not an isolated example; many people the world over come from abusive and neglectful backgrounds. This woman made the decision when she left her mother's home to never drink alcohol or take drugs — and she qualified in social service work to help break her brother's cycle.

The basic needs for her were to find a safe place to live, earn a living to buy food, and have a supportive, non-judgemental community around her. She separated off from her mother's habits and would not give her mother money since she knew her mother would buy alcohol.

To break the cycle is to first see the cycle. This woman realised that she could be functioning with 'more' by witnessing her friend's, family lives.

We all need to be among people to varying degrees. We also need safety, food, water and shelter, we need education for stimulation, and most of us need to feel safe physical intimacy. Once you identify if your early life had serious or even mediocre shortfalls in any of Maslow's hierarchy of needs levels, you may realise you have preconceived judgements, that have constrained you from closing the gap on getting your needs met now.

Introducing the topic of needs is aimed to get you thinking about self-limiting beliefs, and realising your old programme might limit you from aspiring for more. At this point you get to choose how you think about these entitlements. Change requires effort, first attempts may fail, and people's feelings may get hurt as you assess your past needs and establish new desired expectations about getting your needs met now.

The usual time when our needs are unmet is when we are dependent children. We can't choose our family, but once we become adults we can choose our friends and to a certain degree our communities. It can be challenging to speak up about your needs with your caregivers if you are still dependent on them. You could be asking for: respect, tolerance, inclusiveness, understanding, social support, a non-judgemental attitude, or emotional/physical safety. Voicing your opinion and need can be daunting for most people, but eventually you realise that your human rights are intrinsic to your being well and functioning well.

This thinking adds to your personal power. By realising you have needs that should be met, trying to affect change, you are advocating for yourself — and maybe inadvertently others watching from the side lines.

The other big contaminant of unmet need is lack of money, or misuse of money. If we travel back to the story of the woman who as a young person had only marijuana and alcohol on her table, that is both lack of money and misuse caused by her mother's choices. Maybe there was a family history of this type of neglect and/or addiction behaviour that crafted an abuse of money for this young woman's early life story. Her brother was very resourceful by utilising his burglary ability to provide warmth and food. Her resourcefulness was the choice to embrace paid work, which led her away from abuse and neglect.

Money became her saviour, the way out of her past, and saying 'no' to giving money to her mother is her strength. Self-actualisation is at the top of the pyramid, a need that is met last once self-esteem is met. Money gave her the option to reshape her future. Having money is one thing, but taking control of how you spend that money defines your choices and opportunity. Once this young woman had attained her need for shelter and food she then over time could make the choice to help others through her work progression into social service. This direction of meeting her basic needs step by step moved her up the pyramid, achieving her goal to have a partner and children, a purposeful job, and help her brother.

Maslow's hierarchy of needs can skip steps, it's not one directional. A person may choose to live under a bridge, on a benefit or with homeless people because that is what they deem is their supportive community. Their hobby might be collecting 'stuff'; they may visit a church for social support and amenities. This person has met their needs through their choice of bed, location, income, networks and life purpose. Prioritising their system of important needs could mean level three (belongingness and friendship) was more important than level four (esteem) because friendship brings meaning into their life.

The variables and patterns of need are as individual as personality and are influenced by your experiences. Opportunity can be a change maker if you want to change. However this may be influenced by self-limiting belief, microsystem experiences and culture, family experience, connectedness and groupthink. All of these affect an individual's worldview about entitlement.

Money is Powerful

Money is a liberator for some and an expected norm for most people. We are all consumers, and at different times in our lives most of us visit or stay in the land of the financially poor.

Money is a motivator that can travel up Maslow's hierarchy of needs. It can provide for physiological and psychological security needs that allow people to access health care and education, and to build self-esteem and self-actualisation, which is personal growth.

It is important to explore the psychology of money. We view it from different perspectives, and need to unpack our thinking around it, so as not to carry self-limiting beliefs into the future that will hinder our ability to make, hold and respect money we earn.

- Identify family influence around money — how this has affected you, if it is functional or dysfunctional, and how you expect to set yourself free financially.

- An indication of being dysfunctional with money is overspending — finding gratification in the purchase, with no rationale about the consequences.

- Not everyone is good at budgeting, or saving for a financial goal.

- We seem to think that money is a limited resource.

- We seem to resent wealthy people.

- We seem to think that we need money to be happy.

- Some people think it is selfish not to share money.

- The gambler always thinks they'll win it back next time.

Ignorance is a financial crippler. There are a lot of people from diverse backgrounds who are not educated about money. Some have too much money and get given everything they want from wealthy parents. Therefore money seems a given, but in the face of financial change their expectations don't change in regard to wanting stuff. Living within a budgeting discipline is foreign.

Then there are the people who have lived in poverty all their lives. There is evidence that we have generational poverty across families. These people have no surplus cash week from week. They are surviving, and probably visiting a food support agency every week or two. They model to their children that money is restricted.

The credit junkie is the personality that has several maxed-out credit cards. They are always looking for a new opportunity to secure another card or amalgamate cards to ease repayment percentages. They are likely not to make repayments often and suffer the compounding interest. They often don't open their bank mail since they live in denial.

There is another layer of deviant behaviour towards financially challenged people — those retailers who actively stalk and hunt them as vulnerable prey. Unfortunately these deviant businesses hire manpower teams to door knock in low socio-economic suburbs offering stuff, preying on lonely, vulnerable or impulsive consumers.

So again it is important to first locate your beliefs about money from geographical and family influence. If you're in a partnership it is important to also understand your partner's beliefs. Every big town has a budgeting service that will teach you how to budget and save money. I believe this should be a compulsory course for all young people. The life skills of managing money and drawing up budgeting spreadsheets should be taught in all schools alongside maths.

This last section about money has been to unpack your influences and try to establish whether you can isolate the difference between financial need and financial want, and to ascertain if you are on the slippery slope to living in the debt cycle.

Money is a motivator that can travel up Maslow's hierarchy of needs. It can provide for people's physiological and security needs, allow better access to health care, education, self-esteem and self-actualisation.

Section Two - Part 2

Discovering Our Language

Language and Communication

Talking and eloquence are not the same: to speak, and speak well, are two things.

Ben Jonson.

Spoken word, tone, volume, gesture, dialogue and intention is language conveyance that leaves an impression of your views, requests and needs. How you hear other people communicate leaves an impression on you.

The way people use language — whether it be spoken out loud or silently thought, whether it be shared or in writing — is under the spotlight of *Locate Yourself.*

Often our language reflects our family communication style and vocabulary. We are influenced by our neighbourhood, our suburbs, our shared culture, and popular culture trends. Inside all of these influences is the programming of our beliefs about entitlements and aspirations.

Self-limiting thinking is enhanced with language messaging that is negatively geared. Are you self-limiting yourself from welcoming opportunity, relationships, love, joy, fun, health and abundance into your world because the language modelled to you was reductionist thinking? This could be due to stereotyping and narrow world views held by your caregivers, wider family, peers or community.

People have hopes and dreams, goals and needs. They make lists and then rationalise their entitlement — negate or minimise it. They think they don't deserve it or they use words to talk themselves away from their desires. Within this inner conversation are other people's opinions or intentions, sabotaging the attainment of fun, joy, love, relationships, goals, change and desire.

If we are brought up in abusive situations we learn to model this language and social behaviour in order to belong and to stay safe. Our early influences mould us. If the words hurled at you are mostly negative this will influence how you think. If your family is physically dominating you could be reluctant to make decisions. If the words used are abusive you may be passive or aggressive in your communicating style. If your influence was dominated by family humour, your humour may be insulting to others not familiar with your language, tone and humour style.

The ongoing effect of negating language can diminish your self-esteem and confidence. As you move into relationships and friendships you find common ground through language. Sometimes we can be frightened by the tone and vocabulary of others. Moving into new relationships can expose you to confusing communication nuances around praise, humour, put-downs or silence. It is always a challenge being an outsider looking in, and feeling or hearing language you're not comfortable with.

Becoming self-aware of the way you want to be spoken to is very important. Once you realise you have the power to choose what you listen to, conversations to be exposed to, you can minimise a lot of the noise that is agitating your mind and creating stress. This is one of the benefits of mindfulness practice.

When you develop listening skills and compassion you become aware of hurting people's feelings. Compassion is not always a modelled value in some families. Most people will learn this through experience, observation, study and personal response.

Listening is the non-violent practice of hearing someone tell their story, without steering the conversation away from them back to you, or onto something else.

The three components of non-violent communication are:

- Self-empathy — having a compassionate awareness of your own inner experience with communication.

- Empathy — being able to listen to others with compassion.

- Honest self-expression, which is about your authentic self-expression inspiring compassion in others.

Internal Factors - Self-View of the Individual

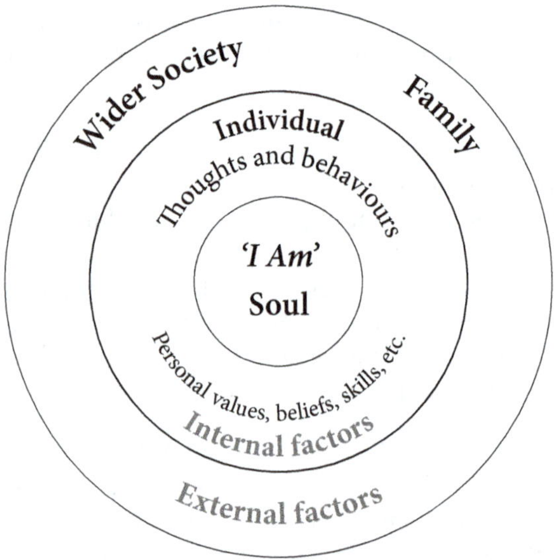

Figure 6

Earlier it was mentioned that personal autonomy is described as 'where do they end and I begin'. If you look at the above simplified ecological systems model you will see that the central two rings are about the *individual*. This area is called the 'Internal Factors' and is the personalised values, beliefs, skills, thoughts and behaviours of the *individual*. Within the core of this central ring will be the *essence of the person*, which is the soul feeling of the *I Am* of the *individual*. This is the place that archives any hurt that runs too deep, that is too confusing for cognitive processing, or that is lost in translation with the self-explanation skills you have at the onset of the original hurt. The *I Am* also holds the feelings of self-love, shared love, love being given, and love received. The state of love is pure nourishment of the *I Am*.

Freud's Iceberg Model showed how much larger the subconscious area is under the waterline. This is a place to store the confusion of the stimuli. Some people disconnect fully from the memory of past hurt, archiving it in their recesses of unconscious memory. Others bypass this area and store it in their body physiology, resulting in reactions like: reduced function, fatigue, pain, insomnia etc. (This information is explored further in section three). The *I Am* resides in the subconscious of many people waiting to be freed from their hurt or oppressed history. Body/mind liberation will come with 'releasing' stored hurt.

The essence of hurt may be lost in translation because the words might not be with you at the time, you may not have any explanation offered, your vocabulary might not be extensive enough to describe your feelings and/or experience, or the trauma is beyond processing at the time. It is then stored in archives of hidden memory, possibly labelled: confidential, brutal, shame, unexplained, neglect, or unresolved guilt. The residue is often negative self-talk or self-limiting belief. Both are the explanations and reactions you archive and programme to the memory, and these can influence lifelong personal behaviour, and self-limiting belief.

External Factors on the model (Pg 55) are positioned from ring three outwards and encompass interpersonal systems that influence an *individual's worldview*. The individual develops language skills — both verbal and non-verbal — primarily from caregivers, then language crosses the systems throughout the life cycle. Another way of saying this is that interpersonal language is the process where people exchange messages, information, meaning and feelings both verbally and non-verbally.

Having identified your worldview, as opposed to the worldview influences from your surrounding systems, it is now time to suggest that your worldview and personal self-view could be tainted with unconscious self-explanation of confusion around hurt memory. This would result in negative self-talk or self-limiting belief about yourself, about other people, or about your circumstances. You may also have developed a distorted self-view, causing overcompensation, over-optimism, people pleasing. The focus now is to become aware of your predominant thought pattern.

Self-Talk

Intrapersonal communication is a person's self-talk. It is internal dialogue that is thinking, reasoning, problem solving, self-explaining, and rationalising. Intrapersonal regulation can be challenged with self-talk chatter that favours the negative aspect of reasoning, thinking, rationalising, and self-explanation. It is usually about talking yourself out of praise, compliments and opportunities because somewhere hiding in your psyche is low or no self-worth. This transpires in lack of confidence, stress, anxiety, and fear reactions. Examples can be:

Outward Action	Self-talk Reaction
Ann says she would like to be your friend.	Nobody really likes me.
Wow, your photos are amazing.	I am always fat in photos.
Congratulations on your job.	Nobody else wanted it.
Hey, Drew is going to ask you out.	Me? No it's a mistake.

The topic is vast and this list only scratches the surface of self-talk. Your exercise is to begin to locate yourself in your inner dialogue in order to find patterns that need changing. Over time, with alternative thinking discipline, you can begin to replace negative thought patterns with positive alternatives. You will then be able to re-programme your thinking and self-talk style to heal buried hurt and/or reshape self-belief programming that would otherwise limit your forward journey through life.

There are many talk and cognitive change therapies that guide personal change. Cognitive Behavioural Therapy (CBT), Dialectical Behaviour Therapy (DBT) and Neuro linguistic Programming (NLP), are only a Google search away, offering a deeper, more detailed explanation. If something resonates with you in the search, then use your intuition as a guide to find a book or a therapist to take you further along this self-discovery journey. But before you put your puzzle together you must locate all your pieces within your beliefs, feelings, intuition, conscious awareness and behaviours. As you join the dots of your life, your subconscious 'stuff' will slowly come into your conscious awareness to be met with your increased understanding of your life story thus far.

Mindfulness Language

Close your eyes. Fall in love. Stay there

Rumi.

Practising mindfulness is stillness in love. Meditation and yoga practice replaces self-talk chatter with stillness. Both together are soul nourishment. Section four offers further explanation of the mindfulness meditation matrix. For now let us focus on the power of mindfulness language freedoms which are soothing lullabies for your mind and soul. Mindfulness language is practising compassionate awareness through language. Both meditation and yoga practice stem from India and Eastern philosophy, the backbone being the practice of breath work and silence. When you concentrate on breathing in and out rhythmically it becomes difficult to maintain mind chatter. This inner dialogue initially has more power than stillness. Most people don't make the connection of how their inner chatter rules their thinking with self and others. Mind chatter is language to self.

Our thoughts control our intentions. Mindfulness practice slows the mind and opens up space to reposition thinking and spoken language. The Vedanta is one of the six orthodox schools of Hindu philosophy that promote Satya — the Sanskrit word for truth, extended into an ethical concept of virtuous truthfulness in one's thought, speech and action. This thinking is echoed in Buddhist values located in the five aggregates, focusing on conscious choice. The origins of mindfulness are one part of the ascension process of enlightenment. Modern and popular practice is initially a change of thinking to move beyond ego and self, to practice speech, thought and action with compassion for self and others.

Mindfulness extends metacognition, which is simply 'thinking about what you are thinking'. With mindfulness, we choose our thoughts to be compassionate and intended, underpinned by loving kindness and gratitude. Its effect is similar to how the audible and inaudible reverberation of Tibetan bowls, church bells and gentle flowing water deliver calm resonance.

Practising release of past hurt by using language is a repositioning in your personal power. Just as language hurts, it also heals. Of course hurt and confusion manifest for all of us differently, just as our stories are our own, so there cannot be one great fix — just tools to implement and to reposition our historical processing and effective healing on. Rhonda Byrne's book *The Secret* encourages readers to reposition their thoughts and language to manifest change at a personal level. It also demonstrates thinking language that has a predominantly negating effect, holding a person in a self-perpetuating cycle of less than what they truly desire. The power of our thoughts creates our reality; we are what we think. Therefore if we discipline the mind by learning to be a witness to our thoughts and inner dialogue, we can locate our thought patterns and begin to think positively and compassionately, and ultimately re-shape our thinking with intentional vocabulary.

Language is a powerful tool when you understand you have positive and empowering word choice, that can be implemented within your intrapersonal and interpersonal conversation, and that will contribute to and benefit your future wellbeing.

Affirmation

Affirmation is said to be the action or process of affirming something with encouragement or emotional support. Affirmation is an intervention that can be the catalyst for personal change. Such change can come from the unexplored potentials in the person, or from social systems. Examples are motivational sayings within a weight-loss programme, or the rituals used at an Alcoholics Anonymous Meeting. Affirmation can change the perception of an individual. The environment may remain static or oppressive, but the individual gains a different internal power to manage this.

Yet not all environments change nor people. Seasoned disarranged people will have defence mechanisms installed as self-protection barriers. Affirmation will seem like a lie to these people. The affirmation fairy will not be trusted. People with low self-esteem in core areas will have built their impenetrable walls. Word cues will be unbelievable until they are ready to absorb them through repetition.

When we think of affirmation we think of words, yet affirmation can be actions. A sense of personal value, purpose, accomplishment and praise in the work/school/arts/sport/skill or task domains can lift self-esteem. Praise in one area will bolster personal integrity that can alter or expand a person's worldview. People want to be recognised as valuable, but for a disarranged person they need to establish a beginning to see the value in themselves, because this developmental building block has been tampered with somewhere in their life journey. Someone telling you that you're good at something is very different from actually realising that you are valuable because you're good at said ability or task. This might be why some people struggle with accepting or believing compliments.

Self-affirmation re-enforcement occurs with repetitive experiences of being adequate at simple tasks. The self-talk that acknowledges the positive execution of simple tasks then builds belief. Once the person believes they are good at various basic tasks they build their self-esteem, which then can be reinforced by external witnesses, and the value of worded affirmation can at last penetrate the protective barriers. This becomes a seesaw that slowly finds its balance. Developing language skill and confidence should promote stronger coping and resilience skills, which will then orientate social judgement, behaviour and self-judgement that have previously been devalued by an eroded self-view. The ongoing development of affirmation belief and personal change will help orientate constructive management of any threat or criticism instead of reverting to minimalising, submission, inaction, or the enablement of negative behaviour, tyranny and lies.

When you have located where you sit within your language output and input, you begin to understand how language affects your decisions, beliefs, actions and behaviours. You take your power back and reassert it with affirming word choice. This is a shift in language and personal-value perception that radiates inwards towards the *I Am* of your person. The new-found understanding and growth enables increasing self-esteem and evolving confidence, which then radiates outwards across the external systems you interact with. This sends a message that changes the trajectory of a person's life course, and can model empowerment options to others on the peripheral who also want inspiration and permission for self-growth.

Word Mastery

Why do some people play self-talk 'tug of war' with personal change words?

Realise that you are the driver of your self-empowerment and healing journey. Emotional conflict can be created with challenging self-worth vocabulary. Emotions are comprised of feelings, and words describe feelings, so each descriptive word has an essence that holds an intention. Therefore emotions have an energy that is flowing. It becomes a choice of how you consciously use your words. Whether spoken out loud or used in self-talk, such words can be positively uplifting or self-destructive.

Psychoneuroimmunology (PNI) is an exciting field of health science that connects the interaction between the human mind and the immune system. It is the science that will validate what complementary therapy has understood intuitively without the scientific research.

The human body has a healing system and the immune system, which are different, but both systems are affected by negative and positive human thought, emotion, feelings and attitude. Emotions are connected to the endocrine system, which controls and releases hormones. Therefore by making better word choices you can improve your health trajectory. (Psychoneuroimmunology is way too big to open up in this book — undertake your own Google search for a detailed explanation).

A disarranged person is in conflict with their personal value. Words have been ammunition in the past. Navigating the emotions of cruel words will challenge some people. Take the power back from words that have left you weak.

Activity:

Listen to your inner language — identify positive, negative and neutral words. Replace one negative word a day with an uplifting word conveying the positive message. Always focus on the positive vibe. Over time you will do this without paying conscious attention to your language, and it will flow over into your outward communication for others to benefit from. The action is to 'fake it until you feel it'.

The words explored next are to get you to think about how you invest in yourself. Let them wash over you. As you read them, try to locate your ownership and mastery of their freeing potential.

Resilience

Earlier in section one we touched on the effect resilience has on the person who is trapped to an unpleasant situation for any length of time, and how that person develops an adaptive set of skills to process and survive in this situation that they have no control over or ability to escape from. Resilience is an adaptive function built into your psyche to help you orientate yourself and cope with difficult experiences. Resilience is a good personal trait to celebrate as you embrace life changes; it gives you flexibility and solution-finding skills, and tenacity in challenging situations. You may have learnt to be resilient in adverse situations, but it turns into a personal asset as you move through your life. Resilience is a desirable ability. Own it as yours because only you know how hard the journey was to hone this skill.

Hope

Hope lives in your psyche just behind resilience. Hope is the shadow that trails the coping mechanism of hardship. At times we all shut our eyes and escape into hope that this saviour, situation changer, person, love, health, shelter, food, money is on its way. Desperate people know how to invest in hope. Yet when you hope you are waiting. We all know waiting can go on forever. Make hope an action word. Change hope to expectation with an affirming action — say *'I expect'* this saviour, situation changer, love, health, shelter, food, and/or money is on its way to me.

Words can be very powerful. Reframe your language as you set your wishes into action. When you change your words you change your belief about your deservedness. Are you worthy of expecting good things? *Yes, you are worthy of your right to live beyond hope.*

Forgiveness

One of the hardest words for a person to embrace is *forgiveness* Why? Forgiveness implies you minimise the injustice, the cruelty, the humiliation, the violence, the unfairness, the hardship, the abandonment, the torture and the lies. Humans hurt each other forever. The only person who can change from being a victim forever is you. Yes terrible things happened, and the reality is you remain a victim every time you relive that personal pain. Forgiveness was the long-awaited saviour in my story of hurt. When I realised the liberation of letting it all go, I knew the effect of healing on my mind and soul. Change yourself, not them…

Can you locate yourself in this scenario?

The person who carries the baggage of past hurt looks tired. The person has tied a half-empty, grey-plastic shopping bag to their body for every hurt they won't forgive. That person continues to live and breathe, but as time goes on they are weighted down by grocery bags. Gradually the accumulated bags obscure the person, who tires of the added weight and starts to lose desire to move, since they are carrying their normal body weight plus all those bags. They are reduced to sitting in a chair all day; they limit their life opportunities to the extent that it has an effect on their holistic health. They stored their hurts — carrying them everywhere, and reliving the hurts to anyone who would listen — and finally no one wanted to be around them.

Learn to Forgive

> *Forgiveness is the fragrance that the violet sheds on the heel that has crushed it.*
>
> Mark Twain.

Practising forgiveness can be as simple as taking a bag off your body and looking at the contents and saying "I forgive you, goodbye" because you don't want to carry the burden around. It doesn't serve you well, so release it into an imaginary rubbish bin or fire pit. This is a simple technique for establishing a forgiveness routine to free you up from carrying unwanted baggage.

The merit of forgiveness is the lightness you live with; you get to a point when hurtful things are said and you instantly ditch it as toxic waste that belongs to the other people. This becomes a natural reaction; if something is particularly cutting you may hold it for a day or two but you soon feel it weighing on you and dump it as forgiveness develops into an innate skill.

It is advisable to work with a counsellor to help you through the layers of forgiveness practice to find personal freedom. Forgiveness is about choosing not to remain a victim to other people's cruelty and opinions. I embraced meditation and noticed a change in how I reacted to processing hurt; when something crazy happens and I'm reaching for a solution I enter the stillness of meditation to find clarity of action. Other people use exercise or prayer for that processing time.

Praying is intention, requesting, thanking. Meditation is clarity in hearing the answer.

The message here is to embrace the power of forgiveness as early in your life as you can.

Fear

If you struggle with forgiveness in your life then I suggest you consider fear as its rival. Fear can freeze us and establish a functioning pattern of survival. To be ruled by fear is not to be a free person. Fear will override any attempt at forgiveness. So how do we recognise fear's grip on our thoughts?

Activity:

Sit in a quiet undisturbed space…Quieten your mind and body… Close your eyes…Breathe slow, deep, even breaths for ten minutes… (You may need soothing music to assist this peaceful state)…Once you've achieved this, even for ten minutes, remember that feeling. That's your neutral, a place of calm.

From this state of calm you intention forgiveness thoughts to the memory that is holding you stuck. If you get a bit of an emotional wobble, that's normal and to be expected since you are releasing something that has caused you past pain.

If the feeling that greets you is intense and forces you against an emotional wall… well, that's fear, so we need to unpack it before we can forgive.

We need to separate fear into two categories. The first category is if you are in fear of a real danger, either a physical or emotional threat. This is genuine fear and needs safety assurances. The category of fear that we are working with here is old fears that created maladaptive memories and that now play forward in self-restriction over opportunities and/or relationships. Fear is a metaphorical prison that holds you away from emotional and physical freedoms.

The realisation that fear exists in the memory of the event you want to forgive is the first step in taking back your power from the memory. You need to explore the memory and write down the fear attached to it. Now realise the event is in the past; it can't re-hurt you. Remove the fear thread in your mind — visualise a pair of scissors cutting the fear thread off the memory, and watch the thread become redundant.

Anger

Anger is such a constructive emotion when you're healing your emotional deficit. Anger is sold to us as a negative emotion, and it can be when you experience other's outbursts of anger. In healing work your past reluctance or suppression to voice anger can often be the reason unwellness has manifested itself, and can be the remedy to release you from the fear that restricts your ability to forgive. So anger used positively towards fear threads will help re-balance your personal power.

Desire

It's never too late to become what we might have been.

George Eliot.

We are all different — our foundations are different, our aspirations are different, and our worldview is a combination of our unique personality and the ecological systems that influence us.

Most people are like meerkats, sticking their heads out of holes, looking far and wide. However when attention is on them they retract back into their holes, hiding among the expected values of their immediate community norms.

Humans are motivated to live, and they are motivated to avoid pain. Beyond survival most people are scared to desire more, be more, do more, and get more. For some people personal aspirations are similar. Chances are they lie just beyond attainment because the drivers — motivation and aptitude seem to lie dormant.

The degree of motivation varies from person to person, depending on personal awareness factors such as: optimism, resilience, self-deserving belief, external and internal resources, health, and personal desire. We are initially moulded from the ecological systems that influence our worldview belief and positioning. In order to grow or expand in a new direction we may need to step away from those holding us rigid, imposing on us their beliefs and conditioning.

Not everyone is a champion, a Nobel peace prize winner, a valedictorian. Yet everyone has the potential to excel, motivate and inspire others to be great at being present, stable and kind. Such people serve humanity in ordinary, simple ways by executing tasks with calm, respectful thought, showing consideration for the person who is benefiting from the shared energy exchange.

This flow-on effect is the magic you leave. That's where you become interesting to others because by default you make others feel good. The book *The Fred Factor* illustrates how an American postal worker inspired millions of people just by the care he took delivering the mail to his community. Unknowingly he became the inspiration for the author Mark Sanborn to address corporate companies on how to treat their customers and employees with respect. Fred the postman became inspirational just by having an interest in relationships on the other side of his mail-boxes.

When you reset your foundation and extend your worldview to think about the value you now have invested in your own story, you then inspire others to do the same.

Section Three - Part 1

Owning Our Health

Health Path

Seek the wisdom that will untie your knot. Seek the path that demands your whole being.

Rumi.

We begin section three by reflecting on the concept of locating yourself. In section one the focus was on understanding the blueprint of the first foundation learned and absorbed from immediate family and wider community influences. An individual can then use self-analysis to redesign a new foundation to build their improved life situation and legacy on.

Section two introduced worldview exploration, which is the concept of understanding where individual thinking originates, and encouraged you to unpack that thinking in alignment with current personal beliefs. This section also touched on topics that open the reader to recognising self-limiting belief, which can impede the progress of setting up a better foundation.

The third section you are entering has a health focus. You, the reader, are now being guided into using lenses of first foundation, new foundation, worldview thinking and critical analysis to locate yourself in your beliefs and past experiences. You can then make new plans about what resonates and will enhance personal re-balancing across physiological and psychological aspects of individual health management.

Simply put, you are encouraged to find yourself within your health history, your family health history, identifying generational saboteurs, cultural beliefs, power imbalances, mental and emotional health, and physical health assessment. The focus is on improving your future health plan and the health legacy you model to family.

Health is an illusion afforded the ignorant. At any time injury or illness can change the trajectory of a life plan. Investing in your health is a journey to better long-term health. It makes sense to revise changing health beliefs and micromanage health goals as you transition through the aging stages.

We need to set health goals and checklists because without them we have no projected health destination to get to, and no plan to improve on our current environmental, genetic and biological determinants. The goal of optimum health is not just a healthy body and mind, but a healthy life. This should be prioritised as a must, not an option.

There is a diversity of health-care options beyond the Western Biomedical Model of health diagnosis and management — psychodynamic therapies, the alternative Eastern approach of diagnosis and treatment, plus complementary and indigenous therapies. All these therapies have the potential to work individually or in conjunction with other health specialities.

Health care is administered to the masses from a variety of providers. Medical doctors and specialists diagnose issues and administer treatment using the biomedical model, which assumes mind and body can be treated separately. This model focuses on the presenting symptoms and pathology of the illness, the focus is on curing the dis-ease. This works flawlessly for most patients.

Eastern medicine and complementary therapies integrate mind and body assessment into the overall diagnosis. Spiritual and psychological dimensions form part of this whole-person approach to diagnosis and healing.

Medicine is evolving. There is a trend that doctors are adding alternative therapies to their medically trained toolkit. Yet the mainstream medical profession is reluctant to change since it holds the power of both diagnosis and the remedy pathway on offer, albeit with restraints due to government policy, funding decisions and waiting lists.

There is a growing need for individuals to take ownership of their physical and psychological health care options. Taking an interest in your personal health history is the focal point of this section. The intention is to get you to locate yourself within your health thinking and observation across the myriad of experiences you have already had. You need to realise you have the personal power to manage your current and future health care. This section will make you think about indigenous health care, nature healing and psychodynamic exploration, among other approaches that complement mainstream medical assessment and intervention.

You are a health consumer who can choose from orthodox medical treatment, alternative therapies, health stores, nutrient support, copious amounts of healthy food knowledge and fitness communities, self-help reading, mindfulness, and tools to assist in maintaining balance. This is personal empowerment when you take the stance to be proactive in your health care.

Body and Mind Constitution

When people are confronted with extreme loss or debilitating pain, most manage their crisis from a practical task perspective. They may get medicated support, utilise a holistic approach or ignore everything. Sadly, some people are not in a position to process it at all.

There is opinion that ignored traumas, big or small, can accumulate in your physical body and/or affect psychological health. This is noticeable in post-traumatic stress disorder diagnosis, and can be the precursor to addiction behaviour, fatigue or autoimmune disorders. It also displays in anxiety and depression symptoms, ghost pains, travelling aches and non-specific pain symptoms.

Practitioners of traditional Chinese medicine, Indian auyvedic medicine, and homeopathy assess a person's health using constitutional evaluation. Essentially the observation is that a person's constitution is their inherited and acquired physical, emotional and intellectual makeup. An evaluation will consider a person's presenting symptoms of illness, food preferences and intolerance. The therapist will look at fears, physical appearance, weak areas of the body and mind, and extend further within each doctrine's assessment speciality.

The following example of constitutional processing is my personal story of how my skewed perspective disarranged my self-worth. The ramification of this is that one morning in my mid-twenties I was faced with an inability to fully use my legs.

I was at a very happy stage in my life — emotionally secure, physically secure, relationship secure, and I was healthy and fit. I had been working my whole life to be at this place of security and personal calm. And now I couldn't move my legs. Having a holistic understanding and a sense of inner knowing, I realised I had been shoving the multiple abandonment of my adoption somewhere because I simply couldn't handle the emotional assault on my reasoning sensors.

My adoption story is that I was adopted at nine months old. For the first nine months of my life my carers were nursing staff who met only my physical needs. This then set the trajectory of how I attached to and trusted people throughout my life. When I was twenty I found my birth mother, which was exciting since I had a romantic notion that it would be a fairytale reunion. Sadly, at the meeting she chose to not want me in her life. That second abandonment was devastating on my self-worth, my self-value and my soul.

Six years later my birth mother reached out with a letter asking to meet me. I was wary because I couldn't handle the emotional violence again. I lowered my guard of protection and agreed to meet her. She didn't turn up. This happened two times in that year, each time multiplying the emotional devastation. Not knowing how to process these rejections, I carried on living my life, hiding the adoption story because all that rejection is humiliating and crippling. When my legs stopped working I had enough knowledge from Louise Hay's *You Can Heal Your Life* book and the support of an adoption advocate to explain its connection to my adoption crises.

I reached out for help and the adoption advocate took me on a journey that was swift and full of tears and explanation, and included the gift of a wonderful book, *The Primal Wound: Understanding the Adopted Child* by Nancy Verrier. Nancy Verrier's passion to understand the behaviours of her own adopted children fuelled this comprehensive research thesis on the trauma experienced by such children. Within two weeks of not being able to physically walk far I had unpacked my story, reframed it, and restored my self-worth. I even learnt to openly share my story to help other adoptees and their partners understand the complexities of an abandoned person. And I could fully walk again.

This crippling experience alerted me to how I'd learnt to cope with my abandonment — my mind was strong enough to file it in my physical body's too-hard basket. Over the years I stored other trauma experiences in my body. Luckily I was aware of my pattern, and knew how to unpack stuff before the severity of ignoring the signs jeopardised my health. I have also seen this pattern emerge with some of the people who have trusted me with their stories.

I liken this to the famous Leaning Tower of Pisa in Italy. The tourist attraction is celebrated for its unique balance. Our human foundation is how we interact with all around us, and we present ourselves from that point of balance. Some of us start from a place of imbalance and build our interactions from that skewed point. Our behaviours and self-belief come from habitual imbalance, but we are judged on them with people assuming them to be part of our personality.

My foundation began with a lack of attachment to my adopted mother. This could have been rebalanced had she known about attachment theory. I was lacking cognitive bonding processes compared to babies who attached to their birth mothers. Attachment is established through the senses, formed from emotional and physical time together. The position I held in my adoptive family was third. My new mother fell pregnant not long after I was placed in the family and birthed a baby who had complicated health challenges, which demanded her full attention. I am fortunate to have been adopted, but the lack of conscious bonding always affected our relationship.

I used to tell people I came from a sea of dysfunction: adopted, mother on antidepressants, separated parents, mother who found therapy in shopping, mother who left the family unit for months on end, poverty… the list goes on. But through my work on other people's stories my own story came to be normalised because I realised other people are exposed to family interactions, often worse than mine. We all come from a sea of dysfunction. Hence we are mostly disarranged. But the knowledge you gain to understand yourself and your early life can become the change maker in your own story and the legacy you offer your children.

This is why I ask you to evaluate your foundation to see if you can try to straighten it up or at least understand why you are leaning like the infamous tower. Assess if you have pains in your body that are affected by past hurt, or are triggered by family members or particular situations. Assess your emotional response or ability to cope around similar triggers. Humans have a natural predisposition to try to avoid being re-hurt.

Self-Awareness

How you assess where you fit by working through this book is only the beginning of unpacking yourself or helping someone else. It's fine if all you get is recognising that the body can store your emotional baggage — that your mind can go a little anxious with processing seemingly small challenges, making you lose emotional coping ability. Or maybe when you reach for something addictive to avoid stuff you might now ask yourself, 'Why do I do this?' You are becoming self-aware.

This is an important assessment skill, allowing you to check in with yourself, your feelings, your inner balance and your physical health. Why? Because you're the caretaker of yourself. No one is ever going to be as close as you to knowing what wellness feels like for you. Once you have mastered this you will know what your off-balance looks and feels like. When you're good at this you can share with your family, friends or colleagues how you balance yourself and be empathetic to others when they are off-balance. (Section 4 is where many balance tools are to be found — but don't jump ahead because you will miss the reasoning for why the tools are beneficial to your body, mind and soul).

Anxiety and Depression

Every person experiences anxiety and depression. Some people experience severe bouts of both, while for others it's an occasional and more minor event. Both respond to any or all of these: friendship and coaching, self-help tools, specific nutrient support, complementary therapies, and a visit to the GP to get some pharmaceutical assistance.

Anxiety is normal reaction to stress or panic. A human faced with danger reacts with fight or flight responses, which elevates the hormone adrenaline. Over time a person constantly dealing with danger can stay in hyperarousal, which may present as heart palpitations, fear of something about to happen, and a state of agitation and panic. Given rest time between episodes the body's nervous system calms down and restores itself. But if the fight or flight episodes are happening daily there is the chance that a person will get stuck in the panic mode, creating an overburning of the hormone cortisol that helps balance adrenaline. This overburning of cortisol puts pressure on the adrenal glands.

Anxiety left unchecked can lead to depression, which can have many triggers. It may be a genetic predisposition, or caused by a medical condition such as hypothyroidism, Parkinson's disease or a cancerous growth. It is usually a cumulative effect of prolonged or overwhelming intense stress, body pain, and internalised anxiousness, due to experiences such as grief, sadness, illness, unexplained pain, crises, rejection, aggression, withdrawal, death, loss, change, failure, humiliation, shame, abuse, fear, expectation, pressure, exclusion, separation, isolation, disappointment and biochemical imbalance. Any of these can be catalysts of doom and despair, either acting alone or combined with others. These combined stresses may be overlapping so it can be difficult to identify where the ability to be happy diminished and identify what triggered it. This is why depression is referred to as being in a black hole of despair.

Most people experience depressive episodes, and these are usually linked to a cause or event. However when there is a prolonged inability to shift from the depressed mood to a genuine daily practice of joyfulness or contentment, the depression reaction is overriding the person's ability to find balance within psychological regulation. There can be a difference to the length of time we journey through the mood cycle to healing, and this is based on the difference between having an optimistic or pessimistic personality. The pessimistic thinker leans towards 'learned helplessness' when they feel powerless. Their self-talk and thinking reflect loss of motivation and an unwillingness to try due to believing they will not succeed or change the outcome. Learned helplessness may have been the modelled coping personality from their foundation influence.

At this point you may need to consider the stigma attached to depression that can jeopardise your or other's healing. If you are vulnerable to depressive moods, investigate possible triggers, and share your feelings with someone in person or via social media. If there is no one you trust enough to share your story with, do a Google search of helplines and mental health internet forums that offer self-help tool suggestions for changing mood chemistry. If you are witnessing someone else experience extreme stress, anxiety and/ or depression, help them by talking to them about help, or get them involved in a distraction activity. This could be the first positive change-maker to their wellness.

It is important to note that wellness tools are very important, and they are covered in more detail in the following tool section. These tools are a first-responder kit, much like an ambulance has the gear to save your life but is not set up for a full-blown heart transplant. Being self-aware means having your self-care at the top of your health priority checklist. This will include a comprehensive list of things that de-escalate your stress levels, things that help you find inner calm, things that make you laugh, things that make you feel connected to the love of others, and places that connect you to the healing magnificence of nature.

When a person is experiencing emotional fatigue it can be hard to digest the helping words of a friend or support person. At worst the helping person can be seen as antagonistic to the person experiencing panic, and may even create conflict that can escalate the already anxious person. Sometimes silence and watching from a distance is support enough.

However as mentioned above, the ambulance is not geared up for heart surgery and there are times when self-help tools must take a back seat, with the person needing clinical diagnosis, appropriate medication, and possibly to be mandated to a care facility. It is hard for people to understand their emotional functioning, their story, their wellness, and their need to be medicated. Medication has an important place when there is biochemical imbalance, particularly in cases of self-harm, or if there is any indication of harm done or intentioned to others. Prolonged depression is dangerous and can lead to suicidal ideation and homicidal ideation. When a suicide death is announced, everyone feels the pain of the hopelessness that person must have felt, and people close to them question themselves endlessly about what clues went unnoticed. The irony with depression is that when a chronically depressed person lifts their functioning or is perceived to be happier it can be simply because they have become comfortable with an intentioned suicide plan.

Developing Addiction Behaviour

How do we cope with abuse, neglect, absent parenting, work pressure, expectation, grief, emotional confusion…? The list goes on, much like the triggers for anxiety and depression. Some people develop distraction, numbing, or denial rituals to find escape and management of life. Addiction behaviour is a ritualised dependency and numbing, which can have roots in childhood loss and trauma. There can also be a genetic predisposition.

Addiction is using substances or addictive behaviours to distract or numb your feelings, to the point of craving that fix to get you through another event, week or day. Depending on the type of 'high' or euphoric episode desired, it may become impossible to turn away from once the addict has the urgency or craving.

Unfortunately such cravings can be exploited with sinister intent when people trap others. Once addiction takes a hold, you become its slave both consciously and subconsciously. Again I suggest a Google search for specific addictions and follow Tommy Rosen, he is easily found on the internet and is known for extending the body-mind-spirituality-mindfulness component in recovery teaching.

Some known addictions are listed below:

- Illegal chemical and plant substances and prescription medication, aerosols, glues and cigarettes.

- Alcohol including binge drinking or excessive social and/or daily consumption.

- Food: emotional and binge eating; anorexia and bulimia.

- People: relationship co-dependency; excessive, compulsive, repetitive need to fall in love; compulsive sexual-risk taking behaviour.

- Money: gambling; compulsive shopping gratification; over spending and hiding the evidence.

- Technology: excessive screen time on Facebook, Tinder, porn, or gaming.

Addiction always affects mental health and sometimes physical health. Addiction can be learned from a person's foundation, being the modelled norm of stress management and avoidance. Addiction is lessened when you own up to it having power over you. Twelve-step programmes are very effective across all addiction categories. They are for people living with addiction and people living with addicts. Twelve-step programmes are community driven and are specific to your unique addiction, with everyone working through the various twelve stages supporting each other. They are confidential, and form a safe, trusting community where people experiencing the same type of addict stressors, confusion and frustration can help each other.

Opening a door to ask for help is one of the hardest things an addict can do. The realisation they are losing control or losing support people is shameful for most people living with addiction labels. Even when addiction is unpacked, with triggers identified and support on hand, it's still not a quick fix. It can take years for people to gain control over an addiction.

The process of change can be exited and re-entered as a person lapses in their addiction recovery. Understanding that an intervention can be effective and explanatory is better than not trying at all. Twelve-step programmes are interventions. Counselling, exercise, health foods and alternative therapies are also interventions.

Sweet Addiction

But what about the children who are daily being trained to be prone to addiction cravings in their snack foods, breakfast foods and school lunchboxes?

Obesity can be the result of food addiction. Many children are rewarded, nurtured and comforted with food. Hence the addiction is born in childhood and can statistically predispose the child to comfort eating, bulimia or anorexia nervosa. The quality of food and beverage made accessible to children is often processed, and loaded with sugar, salt and saturated fat. The majority of reward foods are sugar-loaded and this creates the addiction high and crash that people who experience the effect of addiction describe. The sugar in fizzy drinks, energy drinks and juices can form the pathway to the RTD mixes readily available and marketed to young people who are known for having a binge-drinking culture. This pathway can lead to alcohol addiction. It is known that one addiction culture can lead to other addiction lifestyles. When you are young it is deemed okay to be drunk every week, and live on poor quality foods to make budget for alcohol and recreational drugs. Some families provide this culture as their norm.

This is where you look to your foundation and beliefs and decide if you are predisposed to addiction risk. Is addiction a way you escape complex memory, unmet needs, or trauma? Is addiction the way you find fun? Is it a healer, or a helper? Can you discern friend and family influences in regard to addiction justification, habits and ritualistic practice. Cleaning up addiction is a team effort. That is why the social intervention of peer and group support in Twelve-step programmes helps in recovery. Support groups are the backbone of change because the people within the group have first-hand knowledge of the complex nature of the addiction cycle.

Helpers and Healers

Through this writing my intention has been to be a helper and healer for people who give their time to explore this type of self-help guide. I have endeavoured to expand thinking and act like a directory to guide personal enquiry.

Yet I'm aware that not all those people who come into our life story are healers or helpers. Some can be incredibly damaging, confronting and re-violating, taking us back to trauma and leaving obscure scars and open wounds.

I know that these words will trip some readers up. I apologise for this because even the best intentions of trying to help people with a general introduction of varying psychological topics can trigger vulnerable people. If you are confused by any topics addressed within this book please share your concern with someone you can trust to hear your feelings around what disturbs you.

This raises the efficacy of what helpers and healers are, and why they are just that. From my observations a healer can be a song on the radio or a cat spending time with you. It could be feeling the ocean wash over your feet. It could be the healing touch of a child. It could be a kind stranger smiling at you. It could be a professionally trained therapist, or a support group. It is usually someone you have developed trust with, someone who hears you.

It is not someone who talks at you. It is not someone who makes you feel uncomfortable. It is not someone who frightens you. It is not someone who uses coercive power over you. It is not someone who labels you and treats to the diagnosed label without you fully understanding the facts that lead to that diagnoses. It is not always a pharmaceutical cocktail.

You are your healer when you can be actively involved in understanding where you are placed in your health and wellbeing review. Self-help improves self-esteem and promotes confidence with self-advocacy practice. Most people have an idea of where their wheels begin to fall off their wellbeing wagon.

Taking time to reflect on your health history and writing notes in a health journal can locate events, triggers, behaviour patterns and responses. It can also locate environmental toxicity that could be factored in as evidence for the reason you may be feeling compromised.

Once you have ideas that could be triggers, you can work these into a professional or informal consultation because you are now informed in your exploration of why you feel or present as you do.

Not all professionals are skilled across many genres of wellness. They may be trained in a discipline that is too narrow for your needs. Understanding that you need to try to be an active wellness partner with any professional healthcare provider, may seem strange to some people who are used to being told that their presenting symptoms are this or that.

Some professional people who study for several years can form diagnostic bias because they are inflexible about expanding their knowledge to the efficacy of other wellness tools. There can be a lot of egotistical arrogance in lording over someone who is vulnerable and looking for a magic fix or direction.

There is also the argument that vulnerable people like to give their power to others to fix. As you move forward you need to adjust your thinking to realise that you know yourself better than any person you see for help. You are an equal part of your wellness team, and ultimately you will be the facilitator of your wellness care plan throughout most of your lifetime.

How a person can get a balanced overview of an effective self-directed health management plan is to undertake a self-review of their biological, psychological, social and spiritual balance componentry using a visual template.

8

Section Three - Part 2

Finding Our Balance

Biological Psychological Social Spiritual... Balance

When the best leader's work is done the people say — we did it ourselves.

Lao Tzu.

Throughout this text you have been guided to unpack your life story, and then you have been guided to wade through the hoardings and sort the needed from the unneeded baggage you carry in and on your body, mind and beliefs.

Now you are being encouraged to understand the biological, psychological, social and spiritual dimensions that define how you manage this.

Homeostasis is described as the state of stability or equilibrium. Equilibrium is composure and balance within the body systems. From a physiological point of view homeostasis is critical for survival. Our body systems have narrow tolerances, examples being our need for oxygen to breathe, water to drink, and temperature regulation. Our bodies are continually changing, as are our emotions and our mental processing. This change is a constant throughout the life cycle.

Balance is vulnerable to change. Too much change disrupts our inner balance while too little creates stagnant energy. Change also is delivered via outside influences from our environment and communities. Our routines and reactions create habits that can support or sabotage personal equilibrium.

Optimum balance is walking on a tightrope between your biological functioning, your psychological processing, your social and kinship connections, and the componentry of a spiritual practice.

You need to own your personal awareness of how your balance looks, as is shown with this visual model depicting how the separate sections influence wellbeing:

Self-Assessment Wellbeing Model

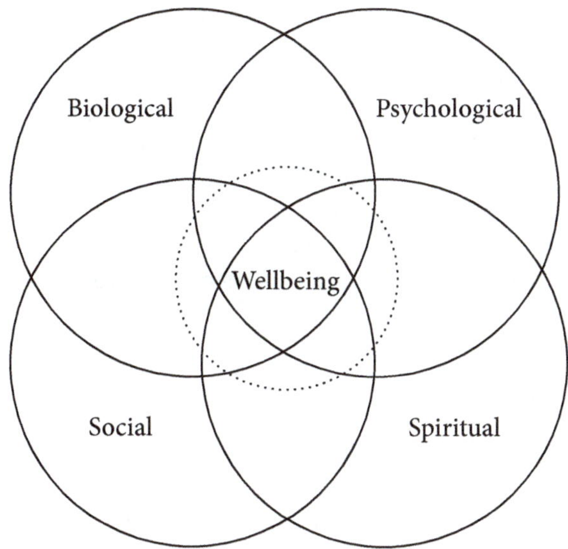

Figure 7

The model forms a visual framework of balanced wellbeing. This becomes your aspiration for personal holistic health management.

The purpose now is to find equilibrium often and quickly, and know like the quote from Lao Tzu, 'We did it ourselves'. Using your self-empowerment and self-care tool you will be able to locate how you are feeling and living daily, weekly, monthly, yearly within your biological, psychological, social and spiritual management plan for health and wellbeing.

We all want optimum health and to function to our full potential throughout our life course. Earlier it was mentioned that not all people have a strong mind constitution or a strong physical body constitution. This indicates that patterns develop silently and subtly, so it becomes necessary to look for imbalance from a proactive self-evaluation and maintenance perspective.

The four components of self-assessment (biological, psychological, social and spiritual) will guide personal wellbeing exploration and definition. Our needs will be unique to our foundation, our worldview, our positioning within Maslow's hierarchy of needs, our physical and psychological health, our capabilities, our goals, our plan, and our motivation to help ourselves. It is individual, and thus works from the inside out to help you interact with your place in the world. It cannot change social injustice caused by others but it can help you become at one within yourself and rebalance quickly when you are rationalising an outside force that's given you a speed wobble. It also gives you an overview of your wellbeing componentry in a visual format that can be shared with any health-care professional you are in consultation with.

In order to understand the four components of self we will look at each one individually.

Biological

The biological refers to the functional things that keep our physical bodies warm, dry and fed. This extends into the physiological processes such as respiration, digestion, elimination, immunology, temperature, circulation and regeneration. The biological aspects are influenced by the environment we are living in, how healthy we are at the time of assessment, and any historical health impacts. You would identify if you are eating a variety of healthy foods, or a diet of nutrient-deficient foods or if you are over-consuming food, alcohol, prescription medication or drugs. Are you taking any nutrient support? Do you have money to stay warm, dry, clothed, fed and secure in a safe space and do you have money to support your social, health and recreational needs? Is your body getting adequate exercise or is it over-exercised. Do you breathe clean air and drink clean water. Do you have access to good health-care providers?

Psychological

The psychological aspect covers (but is not limited to) how we cope with everything going on around us — how we interact with our immediate world. How do we think? How do we manage our emotions, or do our emotions manage us? How emotionally aware are we in the context of others? How quickly do we process change, and find solutions to calm us?

Some people need medical intervention to maintain balance and functioning across the biological and psychological areas. Other people factor in 'me' time and self-care with a variety of strategies and resources. Yet oddly some addictions are created from deemed 'self-care' practices — when used in excess. Overall equilibrium does not stay static — it moves with mood. Any shifts in our environment can trigger sadness, loss, discomfort, pain, social isolation, illness, grief, anxiety or depression. Each reaction is reflective of how an individual copes with change, and is exacerbated if the person faces quick, repetitive or multiple change events.

Social

Our social aspect is how we share our time and space with other people. Do you like people up close or at a controlled distance like an internet forum? Do people scare you? Are you shy or fearful? Do you lack trust in human closeness? Do you become over-involved, over-obligated, and over-loaded with social responsibility? These are important questions to ponder since the answers will dictate how you can find your social balance and the appropriate social support for you. We need to understand how much human interaction we value. How we fit in family groups, friend groups and community groups. How we share time and contact with others, whether human or animal, natural or forced. All these variables define our social tools.

Not all people need people in their immediate world; some prefer animals. People may have been hurt, abused, lied to, over-protected, isolated or unsupported in their history, and these patterns can create maladaptive thought processes about bringing people into their personal space. Regardless of the history, it is possible to balance the social quadrant on the template (page 89) by defining what you like about people and starting to grow healthy, safe tools and belonging from that point of comfort.

Spiritual

The spiritual aspect of this template is very personal and varied. It may include orthodox Christian belief, Shamanic practice, mindfulness, Eastern mysticism or indigenous practice, all of which are influencing people the world over. Faith, spirituality, God, Muhammad and Buddha offer hope, meaning and kinship to those who want this connection. Agnostic believers might spend time in nature to adjust their equilibrium. Again, it is unique to the individual person how they find meaning and balance. Fields, grass, trees, rivers, lakes, mountains and oceans are effectively temples for a lot of people in the world. In times before global urbanisation people lived more rurally and had access to natural resources to balance their souls.

Spirituality can be defined as faith in something outside ourselves — a belief in a divinity that supports us. The use of symbols, music and sacred sites is a pathway towards the ritual of faith pertinent to many belief systems. However there is a wider aspect of faith since it connects us with others who share and celebrate mutual faith as a bastion to ground and support us.

A Zen like Place

This is a brief overview of the bio psycho social spiritual assessment. Interpretation is subjective; the arts, dance, music and poetry can all be classified across most sections. Dance is biologically healthy because it is exercise, but it can also balance psychological health. If the dance is a religious practice it's spiritually healthy, and of course it fits into social health if done with another or a group. But if you don't want to dance for any reason then it becomes out of balance across all sections because you find it uncomfortable.

Homeostasis as mentioned earlier is that state of inner balance across the biological, psychological, social and spiritual aspects of our health and wellbeing. There are degrees of normal and extreme fluctuation to manage. Once you've found a regular place of personal balance, remember it as your happy neutral – a Zen-like place – and you'll more easily manage a route of return after intervals of change and chaos. It is better to make gentle adjustments regularly than ignore the signs of imbalance and have to rebalance with a more radical intervention.

There are always dominant discourses to consider in assessment. Within this framework biological health and psychological health tend to take priority over social and spiritual domains of health. We think psychological health comes first because of the stigma of not functioning, so when were under prolonged stress we pay more attention to staying within the parameters of emotional regulation. We sway within boundaries of balance indicators and have a ready list of things that can return that balance, before we reach for alcohol, pharmacology (prescription or non-prescription) or distractions.

The focus point here is that most times personal psychological imbalance starts in the areas of social, spiritual and biological imbalance before it displays with psychological anger, stress, anxiety or depression. This is why you need to identify existing tools that fit each section and maybe try some new ones from Section 4 to add to your wellbeing toolbox. There is also the added benefit of locating yourself before you look to a trained professional to assess and label an 'illness' or prescribe an antidepressant without understanding you beyond your presenting symptoms. This self-assessment is a road map you can take to an appointment that is also a visual overview of your current 'self-initiated' client-led assessment.

Engaging with the Homeostasis Template (next page) will guide an individual to locate their current areas of strengths and weaknesses within the biological, psychological, social and spiritual components that contribute to their functioning wellbeing.

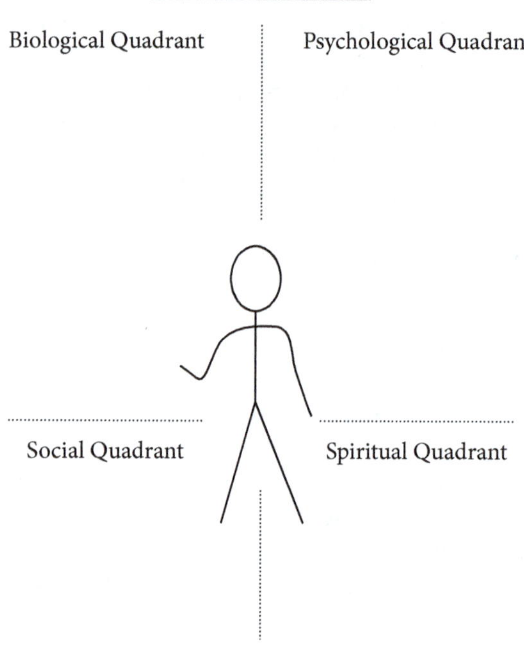

Figure 8

Activity:

Copy the above homeostasis template into your journal. As you read through the Bio, Psycho, Social and Spiritual sections, familiarising yourself with each section's criteria, write the relevant quadrant things that you do from the short list of suggestions. Also add practices that are not mentioned. When you have read all of Section 3 and finished this exercise, total up each section's practice-of-self-care activities. If each section has roughly equal amounts of self-care activities you could say you are generally well balanced in your overall self-care. If one particular section has too few suggestions, then it will be obvious you will need to put thought into balancing that section with suggestions of self-care from the tools discussed in Section 4. However if you have fewer than three listed activities in any quadrant you are under-valuing your personal self-care priority.

The pattern you are locating is also guiding you to think about why one section might underperform or overperform. Often this is to compensate for any variables that may be triggers of apathy in your wellbeing.

Now with a different coloured pen write at the bottom of each quadrant things that you would like to incorporate into your homeostasis plan that you think might be enjoyable, or might benefit your wellbeing.

Revisit this homeostasis template regularly to update new resources that enhance and rebalance your pattern of self-care practice when you feel an emotional wobble taking control.

Purposeful interaction with the template will identify imbalance or balance within each area, telling a story about your pattern of wellbeing. By using this template you begin to do your own work locating areas that need some attention and self-care.

Example: Self-Aware Assessment

Being self-aware and having a visual tool to establish a self-check list of things that work at helping you live a balanced life is something most therapists would suggest you make. I often refer to my own toolkit when things in my life go to the crazy, not-coping basket.

My tippers usually occur in the social aspect and the biological aspect. My strengths are in the spiritual aspect since my meditation practice calms me and identifies where I'm losing balance. If I ignore the onset of emotional fragility with its short-fuse anger and the pressure of mounting anxiety then I have to factor in more recovery time.

How I self-assess my situation is a quick check in with my biological health. Have there been any changes to my diet? Where am I placed within the mood swings of my menstrual cycle? Have I been exposed to chemical or noise pollution? Have I got a visitor staying in my house? Have I been missing my regular exercise? Is there conflict within my family that has been exhausting me? Have I been sleeping well? Am I getting enough nutrient support? Have I over-committed myself to meet the needs of family or friends?

After a thorough narrowing down in the biological area I will check in with my spiritual health and assess if my practice has been honoured. I will ponder if I have nourished my soul with nature. Have I touched the grass barefoot? Have I spent time with the ocean, or lost myself in music? Have I talked with the Buddha, God or a spiritual community of like-minded people lately?

I will then assess the social quadrant, looking to see if I have been socialising. Have I been connecting with children and wider family? Am I spending time with the family pets? Have I had fun with any friends lately? Have I felt part of any community events or gatherings? Have I been too busy in my work, meaning I have isolated myself from sharing time with people who make me feel comfortable and light? Have I been giving too much of myself to people, running my tank dry?

In the psychological health section I will acknowledge if I'm grieving for any loss — a work disappointment, a relationship issue, or the death of a person or pet. I will factor in the effects of disaster and bad news. I will assess any environmental influence. I will ponder any health changes. A change in circumstances in the biological, spiritual or social areas will trigger an imbalance in the psychological aspect of self.

With this assessment I have located my personal default pattern of imbalance — I fall short in the social section. When things become difficult I close out social connections first to preserve my energy to cope. I link this pattern back to my childhood lack of parental support, since both my parents worked and didn't spend quality time with me. This moulded my self-reliance — a pattern of managing my problems alone. This is not unusual for disarranged people in the Western world because the culture around sadness is to not complain but soldier on. What I have learned is that people isolate themselves when they are hurting or struggling. This is a Western cultural idiom that needs changing.

In my own assessment, when I see the isolating pattern from my supportive people having an effect on my imbalance I action a text out, organising coffee dates in cafés to reconnect with great people. I often don't need to share my story because the collective readjustment of my overall bio-psycho-social-spiritual assessment has identified my imbalance locations and I have tried-and-tested sets of fixers in each quadrant for readjusting my equilibrium.

Section Three - Part 3

Connecting With People

Isolating Social Networks

There is a growing trend to look at people through the image they present on social media. This image is manipulated to showcase the superficial connectedness of humanness. Mostly the content lacks substance, with its positive-experience vibe. This is media, and media is preferable when it is newsy and upbeat.

Social media is a great tool of connection, but it misses the nuance of people who are emotionally hurting and prefer to isolate that part of themselves away from helping networks. Now let us expand our thinking on why, in Western society and culture, people want to isolate themselves when they're hurting.

Western family culture has changed and people are expected to work to meet financial need, hence they are busy just surviving. They may miss the silent signs that indicate someone needs a little extra attention because they're not coping with something that challenges them.

The fact that families are fragmented creates physical distance that justifies absence in the care and support role. Beyond family groups are the neighbours who once were classed as pseudo aunties and uncles, and kept an eye on you because you were a fixture of an established neighbourhood. These neighbourhoods have now gone because people are more transitory, due to work choice and career expectations.

When people are busy they reduce the human involvement around them; they choose to not engage with strangers, instead looking past them. By not meeting their gaze they maintain their personal bubble in a more condensed space. This means they refuse to see when they should offer help, but they also isolate themselves from support when they in turn need it.

People reduce their social networks, narrowing them down to work colleagues, peer groups, and occasional family contact. These relationships are generally superficial and lightweight, geared around the group focus. However they can be supportive and tend to be as strong as the emotional depth and group-care ethos invested in them.

Not all relationships are superficial. Some have a richness that reflects time invested by both parties, and some families have bonds that are enviable. There are also those friendships where no matter how much distance and time between connections, each new meeting begins as rich and as full as when you departed the last one, be that three months or thirty years ago. I have always said that some friends are in your life for a short time and others forever, but cherish the value they add to your life, drop any expectation, and live in the moment with them.

With the external pressures dictating scenarios in the lives of many, we need to think about those individuals who have struggled with depressive episodes because their supports are distant and unreachable — because we are busy and think the next person will take up the mantle and do the support thing. Don't assume someone's lined up behind you to carry the load; be that someone.

Help a friend out of despair and know that friendship is forged from care.

Implementing this easy assessment tool to monitor your wellbeing across the four quadrants will make you think about how you connect with people when you are coping with change, hardship or prolonged stress. Society is changing and people are transient and migratory; therefore there are constantly new people settling into communities who are lonely and looking for inclusion in groups, clubs, schools and sport teams.

9

Our communities are becoming diversified with incoming people trying to fit. This geographical homogenisation creates potential new friendships that extend everyone's evolving worldview. There is a tendency for some old established family networks to shut the door on new people because their existing networks are regionally strong. It can be difficult to welcome strangers into established friend groups and communities, but once they have a foothold inside a group they will expand their connections, adding value to both groups, and merging and multiplying social networks.

Moving from the outside of a group to the inside can take years for some people. Within your social quadrant is the need to collect your tribe of helpers, friends, supporters and connections. This is the time to push into established tribes instead of isolating yourself away. Connecting with people and being involved will extend your networks, which can turn into supportive friendships.

Collect Your Tribe

Owning who you are is a destination for people. Knowing when you fit in a group is great. Finding your tribe is satisfying.

How you identify your tribe is based on the unity of sharing, trusting and supporting — growing vicariously through shared stories, activities, challenges and fun. Your tribe is the collective group of people, animals, deities, and networks that you trust, who support you, whom you call friends, who care for you, who listen to you. And who let you care for them in return.

Tribes are the family we collect from our interactions with humanity, which may be with special-interest groups, mentors, social clubs, neighbours, sport interests, therapy groups, internet forums, religious unity, schooling, family groups, pets — the list is endless and abundant.

The tribe is your network of support and belonging, your eclectic mix of people, animals, and resources that have helped you through tough times, good times and ritual times. The motto of a tribe is 'a problem shared is a problem halved'. Essentially the tribe reflects the sub-culture mores of the broader geographic culture... And it is here that established taboos can lead a person down an isolated road.

It is important to be mindful of the cultural difference of men reaching for inclusion and support.

A man's tribe looks different from a woman's. Men can struggle with sharing their personal stuff, their feeling stuff. Being asked to locate themselves within their foundation, their worldview and in their health could seem senseless to a man. Yet there are many men already invested in promoting the need for their male community to take an inventory of their programming, beliefs and health care. This information needs to infiltrate all man tribes to reach the masses of isolated males looking for inclusion and mentoring to clarify and define the traits of a good man.

But before we journey into exploring the difference with the way males do their thing, we need to understand how difficult it can be for a disarranged person to trust people who offer help.

Trusting People

Waiho i te toipoto, kaua i te toiroa.

Let us keep close together, not wide apart.

Māori Proverb.

Learning how to trust people who offer help, advice and comfort can be a challenge for any person. The social quadrant of the bio-psycho-social-spiritual assessment demonstrates the importance of finding people to journey alongside us to improve connectedness, balance and wellbeing. Yet a disarranged person will push away or reject an offer of help.

We are programmed to struggle, keep it private or simply block because our hurt is buried, and our confusion is under self-management.

The flow-on effect from my lack of attachment in my early life reflected in my lack of trust in people. I developed resourcefulness in my problem-solving because the adults were busy with their own struggles. This created a self-reliant, independent and hypervigilant person. These personal traits are considered great, yet my programmed behaviour disabled my ability to trust that people wouldn't hurt me. Therefore the traits were a collection of skills and strengths that stemmed from adverse conditions in my first foundation years.

These traits rendered it strange to ask for guidance or accept help from people. I realised years later how many people saw greatness in me and tried to guide me. These sadly were missed opportunities of mentoring. The mentorships I turned down would have reduced my struggle, and given my life a wholesome, supported direction. Realising I turned potential helpers away because of my default programming makes me sad to this day, because I would have begun my personal healing and trust-restoration work a decade earlier.

This raises the question of how many of us miss the signs of help being offered or turn down support because of our history of damage. We alienate ourselves because of the cocoon that we bind tightly around us to protect ourselves from being re-hurt. And every time something frightens us we weave another layer of protection. We have an invisible buffer zone between us and others. Some of us live with this for life. The problem is that it reduces our ability to heal, to feel, to trust, and to be loved.

The removal of this cocoon of protection can be problematic since it has a mind of its own, and once it starts to unravel it exposes triggers and behaviours that show you are not coping or functioning the way you normally do.

Unravelling this cocoon is cathartic, but the journey through the unravelling process can be difficult and painful. Once you embrace the realisation that you have a defensive cocoon the unravelling starts to weaken the protective glue. You develop insights, fears, feelings, knowing.

An easy way to establish if you have a cocoon is to observe how often people come close to you, and if you project a conscious barrier to stay at a safe physical and emotional distance. You're aware most people seem to attract others, yet you seem to push them away. And you envy how easy it can be for other people to click into new instantaneous friendships within the group situation you are in.

Keeping yourself private and controlling how you invest in the human exchange is a boundary-management skill taught across many professions to regulate on-duty and off-duty roles. The skill is in being able to turn the conscious barrier on and off specific to the environment. The difference I'm talking about with disarranged people is that they have their terms of engagement turned off in most if not all new social settings. It can come across as arrogance, disapproval or aggression, it leads to possessiveness or control of established friendships, and it means the disarranged person can take longer to allow new people into their personal space.

The conscious or unconscious fear of trusting people has a cumulative effect on self-esteem and personal-energy investment. People can blame their insecurities and social behaviours on others for judging them unfairly, but usually the accused people are reacting to unwelcoming facial and body language projecting from the insecure person and simply mirroring that back. (A deeper psychological interpretation and understanding could be garnered by doing a Google search on defence mechanisms, to broaden individual knowledge since the dynamics are deeper than this body of work needs to address).

Uncloaking the stuck layers of protection is a liberating personal process when the patterns start to shift. Healing comes through the dissipation of old thinking and the newness of sharing space non-judgementally, evolving into a personal light-energy of acceptance that emanates positively to yourself and others. What you mirror out is mirrored back as friendliness, and this is an energy exchange that helps you collect a tribe that will stay close to you on your life journey.

Being Man

> *It is better to light a candle than curse the darkness.*

> **Chinese Proverb.**

Yet it is important to be mindful of the culture of men in relation to health, social inclusion, and trust…

This project is about:

- Identifying points of inequality from an individual's formative years forward.

- Trusting that disarrangement programming can change with knowledge to rearrangement, understanding and personal empowerment.

- Trusting that personal empowerment transcribes to better parenting legacies for your children to model to their children.

From a therapeutic perspective, this work is a generic approach to anyone wanting to locate themselves and drive a better future plan, bolstered by knowledge about individual wellness, social inclusion, trust in others, productivity and balance.

This next part is dedicated to the warrior men who dare to be different and question the 'why' and the 'where to from here' understanding of masculinity. These warriors empower more men to question how they feel, and to share their experiences with the emotional stuff, the feeling stuff, the intimate stuff, and the death stuff.

Being female is different from being male; society influences our assumptions on what being male is, as it does on being female.

Sociological gender norms are instilled in babies from the pregnancy stage. We become our gender from role expectations that transcend global culture mores, and obviously our biology is different — anatomically, genetically, hormonally and emotionally.

Men are different from women in the way they deal with their emotional baggage — how they unpack it, when they unpack it, if they ever unpack it — to the point where they may not even think they have baggage. Instead they blame it all on their current partner, past partners, work colleagues, mother, school etc. The list is endless as it is for women. Statistically some men seem to bottle in their disappointments and confusion under layers of distraction and avoidance strategies combined with excess use of alcohol, sex, drugs, porn, work, violence, exercise or cigarettes. This list is not unique to men since women also participate in these activities and both genders are prone to developing addiction. It is plausible that most men process emotions differently, with outwards activity — a keep busy avoidance thing — is more favourable than reflective processing. Women, on the other hand, are known to analyse from the inside, share the disappointment, vent and cry, then use distraction activities to find balance windows and positive emotional shifts.

Babies are born without a gender-belief programme; it is mostly society who assigns a gender-typical role of behaviour. Both nature and nurture influence how the genders become defined. Typically gender is defined by categories such as masculine, feminine and neuter, but there is now a myriad of labels redefining or delineating completely new categories of gender, along with the roles and behaviours therein.

Science states that hormone differences contribute to gender characteristics. Testosterone is the dominant male hormone and estrogen is the dominant female one. Both hormones are present in males and females, in differing ratios depending on gender development and life transitions. Not only do these hormones influence physical characteristics, they also contribute to emotional responses. In traditional societies men were the hunters, and testosterone powered the male to hone his strength and focus on the target of hunting prey for the survival of the wider tribe. He did not have to explain his motivation or his feelings about his role. Fast-forward testosterone programming to modern man, and there is evidence that testosterone affects a male ability to communicate emotion and feelings. The male brain is geared to be brief in explanation and give directives. In traditional societies this worked fine, but these days males are statistically four times more likely to commit suicide in the face of adversity than the estrogen-programmed female. We don't have the suicide statistics for males in traditional society, but I would think they were too busy hunting, breeding and protecting – all physical activities. Men function well from a 'doing' perspective and woman function well from a verbal communication perspective.

We expect men to be hard and strong, and be the aggressors, the protectors, the providers. Young men are programmed from toddlerhood to suck it up with a minor sport injury while girls are comforted for the same injury. Boys are told to stop whinging if their feelings have been hurt, whereas girls are encouraged to discuss this hurt. This pattern develops throughout the child's developmental years and is reinforced by older male role-modelling the hard-man stereotype in sports domains, churches, schools, families and media.

Therein lies the problem with men struggling to discuss or release their frustrations, emotional confusion, humiliation, disappointments, grief and trauma in a rational, healthy way. The older males are modelling an outmoded behaviour that perpetuates on going-silence, frustration, confusion, communication limitation, and bottling up. In the face of crises, instead of seeking wise counsel they hold it in tight and tackle it their own way, or revert to the distraction of alcohol, drugs, aggression or maybe a quick Tinder affair.

Inadvertently men sabotage men's mental wellbeing, with that generational man-speak of 'let's not speak too deeply about feelings'. Women have come through and benefited from the feminist movement that offered global platforms to showcase women's strength and help them gain personal power in the boardroom, sport arenas and kitchens.

Men haven't fully had their movement. There's a beginning. There are many males that have recognised the need to more easily communicate their programmed patterns of behaviour, their need to understand women, their fear of failure.

Paulo Freire coined the term 'dialogical encounter' in his book *Pedagogy of the Oppressed*. He noted that the oppressed don't know they are oppressed within their own community; they stay together, work together and take on the cultural norm of what's modelled for or expected of them. The only way the oppressed are freed is by having conversations with others outside their community. This suggests men need to extend their male networks of wise counsel to other male forums to find personal growth and to more deeply understand the legacy they leave their sons.

With this writing I posit the idea that you grow from your foundation into adulthood, so I'm asking you to question yourself. Am I functioning well? Am I okay? Have I got equity in my relationships? Do I own my thinking? Am I active in my health management? Self-help is difficult for men. They live in the moment and when life deals them a blow they take it on the chin and are reluctant to talk it through with anyone. They are programmed to internalise their emotional stuff.

Most men aren't natural communicators, especially when they are dealing with the big stuff like divorce, illness, unemployment, death etc.

My observation is that men inadvertently cheat other men out of the opportunity to move the silent boundaries of being male, because of an unchallenged definition of masculinity that does not fit with the millennium. The parameters that define masculinity derive from a sociological construct that sabotages men, making them feel they can't be vulnerable, can't expose their sensitive thoughts, health and emotions.

Men fear emasculation, which is the feminising of masculinity imposed by both males and females through actions or words that make them feel less than their ideal of masculinity. They strive to display their muscle mass, intellect, physical strength, earnings, setting up all manner of competition. The reality is we love celebrating these characteristics and thus hold men prisoner to a paradigm that needs to realise it holds men stuck.

The male domain is now diversifying with the main stream acceptance of the gay community, same sex marriage, transgender people and the LGBT community. This verifies that we are redefining masculinity but only on select platforms.

The silence of men kills men, along with the unchallenged concept of masculinity, and society perpetuates the problem with its ignorance. Ultimately we can all make a difference with helping men recognise their need to value their mental and physical health. Fathers need to become uncomfortable in order to make their sons comfortable. Men in communities need to step into fatherless men's lives as mentors, teachers and friends. Women need to back off so men can establish a male community. I personally think that the game changers leading and broadening the concept of masculinity are the young men coming forward since they have more tolerance of difference, and can include diversity in their worldview. I think they model this backwards to the older men, who are becoming the dead wood with their ignorance around the changing face of masculinity.

The outcome we all need is that men can 'walk and talk' their concerns when they feel the shit is beginning to head towards the fan — not when it's already hit the fan and definitely not after it's gone through and splattered on the wall. At this point it takes a lot of effort to clean up. The irony is that women are usually the clean-up crew.

...Men

Are at their most vulnerable when they are in sexual union with a significant partner they trust. Histories, hurts, hopes and plans are traded, while previous friendships become distant. The two become one and then they add children. Time goes on and one day the partner and kids leave. The man's all alone. He traded his male friendships years earlier for this. Sure, he works with men, but he's too shamed to talk about his new-found circumstances. He's humiliated. She's all right — she has family, has friends, talks about her feelings. Him… well, she was his friend, the only one he could be vulnerable with, the only one he talked with about his history, hurts, hopes and plans…

At this low point in a man's life he can statistically be most vulnerable to suicidal ideation and/or homicidal ideation. Women, please understand that a man's community is his saviour; men, please understand that at this point you need to actively make yourselves uncomfortable and talk to another man about the internalised jumble that makes some men feel worthless and confused — the invisible stuff.

…Women

As mothers, partners and carers of males, we need to embrace this new knowledge and think about our current preconceived beliefs about men. Identify when support is needed and how to lead the male horse to good water, and if he doesn't drink, so be it. Back away a good distance because in the silence other males might approach the waterhole, slide next to the vulnerable man, and say 'how's it going mate'? Observe this unique language of proxemics, physical activity and few words — still effective when the dialogue is supportive. Let men be the healers and change makers for men.

And remember that the role of women in traditional societies was to be the gatherer. They foraged for edibles, wove fibres to make better nests, and cared for children and men. In modern times we should strive to gather information, resources, and current research that might be the tools to put in the view of men. Tools can be the difference that makes the difference for any male struggling to understand their foundation, their beliefs and their interpersonal relationships, and to live a balanced life.

Section Four - Part 1

Self-Care for Mind Body Soul

Intuition and Energy

The Future depends on what you do today.

Mahatma Gandhi.

Section four explores expanded thinking around self-care options and practice. People often reward themselves with material items – holidays, spa treatments, foods and experiences. This practice is self-care if it doesn't create a flow-on of stress from the expense or disappointment that can result. Making good choices in your self-care regime is under review in this section. We value our mind and body by identifying our stress threshold, our tolerance limits, our natural resources, and the skills we have that can rebalance, nurture and nourish our physical body, our mind and emotions. We all have a mind and a body; without both we are technically dead. For those with an understanding of energy, the esoteric and indigenous belief we are spirits, souls and ethereal.

Yet this belief that the body ends at the edge of our skin is limiting our understanding of the complexity of our embodiment of space within and beyond the surface of our skin. If we are to honour our understanding of what our self-care needs are, we have to open our minds to realising we are more than the scientific opinion that we physically hold space within the shell of our skin.

Some people are content to believe the body ends as it visually and spatially presents. Others will like the validation that the body has an aura of energy. Because we are discussing self-care it would be discriminating to exclude the topic of energy field existence. Sometimes complete diagnosis is restricted because we don't validate a person's belief. Words such as 'intuition', 'I feel', 'guided', and 'spirit', tell a story about how someone is understanding their information because they are sensitive to this energy.

Energy frequency and vibration enables clairvoyants and mediums to 'read' your field. The fields of energy are like an eggshell emanating from the outer edge of your skin, with the ethereal energy traveling both inwards and outwards.

This is why a person has visions, or a devout practice of knowing, or can tell experiences from dreaming, ESP, déjà vu or past-life memory to name a few.

The Subtle Body diagram (next page) demonstrates the subtle energy fields at play. The diagram is a static representation demonstrating how energy fields present themselves.

The diagram is subjective since it can only exist as it is perceived and is not a true representation in itself. The reasoning is that energy changes with emotions, moods and thoughts. A person sitting in a meditative state in stillness holds their energy fields in a subtle, fluctuating stillness; the stability is governed by the stabilised breathing pattern. Holding space in a higher vibration is achieved with pure, clean energy workers, which could be people like meditators, monks, and priests, or places like beautiful gardens and areas where the forest meets the beach. Such places hold serene energy, which is holding space.

The energy in a space can be frenetic, and is reflected by collective people's energy which is constantly changing with each person's moods and emotions. Hospitals, schools, shopping malls and prisons are dominated by frenetic energy, which is polluted energy. Family environments can be energetically frantic with individual agitation, electronic agitation, and relationship agitation dominating the feeling of the shared space. In relation to the diagram; when you think about the energy emanating off individual bodies you can see that simply by sharing space watching TV, you are sitting in each-other's energy fields.

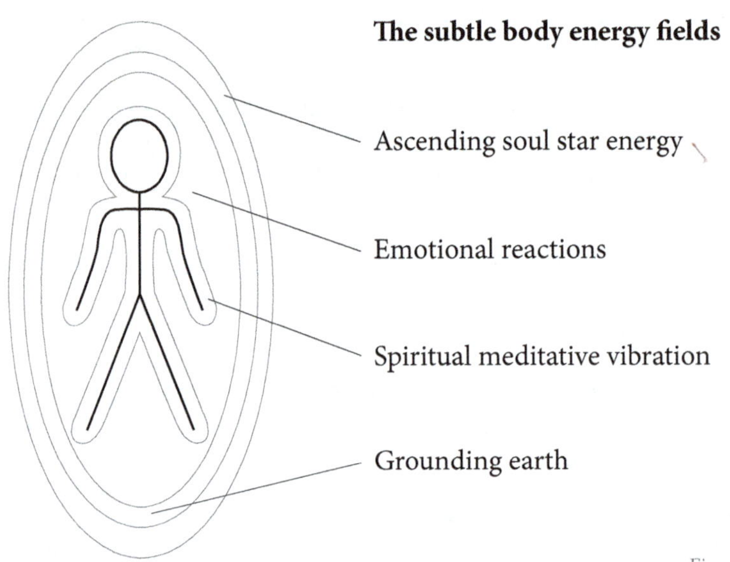

Figure 9

It is important to locate your opinion about intuition and energy belief. This might be something you keep hidden because dominant opinion around you might judge you as crazy. Orthodox religion dominated and attempted to cleanse individual and indigenous spiritual practice of these sensitivities, labelled them crazy and mentally wrong, and created fear and stigma around extended hypersensitivity to energy frequency.

Every living being has vibration frequency variance and emission. This sensitivity is prominent in discourse about why animals react in different ways to individuals. Animals sense fear, harmful intent and kindness. Frequency and amplitude determine the oscillation vibration, which changes with emotion and environmental reaction.

A devout meditation practice can create happy oscillating cells that radiate out as a shimmer. This is described as radiance, similar to the power that sexual orgasm can deliver — again very happy cells, and ironically very good self-care in practice. Sayings like "you're ten percent more or less of the people you associate with" and "like attracts like" reflect the power of energy recognition.

Addiction writer Tommy Rosen says being in the frequency of addiction supports magnetism for addictive behaviours, thoughts and like-minded addicted people. Some people recognise when they have encountered someone who has not long experienced a powerful orgasm, since their cells 'remember' and trigger arousal in the bystander. This reverberation energy is attracting. There is another spiritual energy — referred to as kundalini energy. It is the alignment of spiralling energy vortexes within the chakra system moving in an upwards motion towards Godhead/soul star (indicated on the diagram) and travelling back to ground/earth star. This energy is enlightening and rebalances the individual chakra areas.

Hindu temples are places of worship, and in India they are covered in sculptured demonstrations of sexual acts. Orthodox churches dictate modest sexual criteria for procreation. Both are places of worship and scripture, yet Hindu belief understands the alchemy and pathway of sexual energy as being another way to reach God.

Referring back to the energy body diagram, you can see how the plume of energy radiates out. Normal extension off the body is a half metre, but sustained joy extends the boundary out to two metres. Fear or uncertainty retracts the fields to sit closer to the body, sometimes on the skin surface. Fright has been described as "jumping out of your skin", which is true since the person gasps in air and with audible reaction expels air. This description describes the benefit breath has with calming physical body reactions and breath also stabilises the energy field.

Once realised, energy manipulation can be euphoric. So it is important to note that a comprehensive grounding practice needs to be implemented. Energy is associated with the pineal gland at the base of the skull. Within spiritual thinking this pineal gland is linked to biochemical processes known to promote dreaming and neurochemical interactions that extend consciousness. Meditative states may enhance interactions between the biochemical functions of the pineal gland and the wider endocrine system, producing 'psychic experience'.

However energy is addictive, and is experienced as a 'high' when not understood. Liken this process to a balloon filled with helium gas, left without restraint it will rise up and up. Many meditators can be witnessed as 'floaty' or 'high'. This is because they are floating out of balance. Energy in the mid to lower body is dense — it is like a balloon being filled with oxygen, and it will float and bob close to the ground. Within the energy-teaching communities 'grounding' techniques emphasise the need to keep the meditation balanced in the body. The saying 'as above, as below' is about sending energy down the body into the ground at an equal distance between the head and bottom (feet, if standing). This energy balance is demonstrated in the energy diagram with the space under the feet being at equal distance to that above the head.

Prayerful chanting and music are spiritual practices that intone frequency. Music has harmonics that resonate with individual energy balancing. Used wisely, soft music and chanting build purposeful unifying collective energy. This is why churches and temples instil reverence, so as to hold space and collective energy to commune with God since this frequency enhances a direct line to heavens telephone system.

Spirituality

Faith is the most powerful concept to understand and believe in. Yet terminally ill people facing their own mortality cling to spiritual faith as the last bastion of hope in a possible cure.

What is spirituality? Some would say it's an orthodox religion. Some would say it's the incorporation of the esoteric realm in their belief.

Some would say it's the combination of both of these. Some would say it's communing with nature. Some would say it's losing yourself in a beautiful body of music.

There is no definitive answer since spirituality is unique to how an individual embraces the concept of something sublime yet intangible.

There are people who are indoctrinated into a religion that is the vehicle to their spiritual practice and identity. Some of these people are bonded through a cultural norm and have no choice but to live their faith by rote. Others embrace the fundamentals and explore faith from a broader perspective.

Yes I Am, I am also a Muslim, a Christian, a Buddhist, and a Jew.

Mahatma Gandhi.

There are others who are immersed in nature and animals, and who define their belief in attuning to the seasons and cycles of the natural world.

Others live their faith by volunteering and assisting humanity, seeing a need and offering to walk a difficult journey alongside someone.

It does not matter how you come to incorporate the art of spirituality into your life.

In every type of spiritual practice there are people who have suffered restrictions or abuse administered by people in authority positions. This creates turmoil and confusion because the behaviour of the spiritual teacher, family member or leader is in conflict with the essence of spiritual practice. As a result people move away from spiritual belief in its entirety, since it has a pain memory of abuse and distrust.

Spirituality is love of others and self-love; it promotes inclusion and kindness. There is serenity within spirituality that, once found, forms an inner strength that holds you buoyant in difficult times when other self-care strategies are not enough to help you through.

If your life has dealt you blows and you have lost faith in being held by the energy of something wholesome, the pain you carry is a mix of disbelief, confusion and loss. This is grief; you may be grieving for spirituality you've never experienced in your life, or grieving for a lost domain of spiritual practice that you left for safety reasons.

Faith, music, ritual and spirituality all form the basis of any religious practice. If you are living without a spiritual understanding because of past abuse, non-exposure, or ignorance of something bigger than yourself, then you may be limiting yourself. Once you define what your temple is you can begin to create your belief system by cultivating your rituals, music, dance, art, nature and affirmations. This understanding that you craft your personal temple within yourself is the beginning of finding yourself within spirituality.

In times gone by all humanity was connected to the environment, through rituals, and spiritual practices of blended indigenous belief across the world. Somewhere along the way people placed spirituality in the 'not necessary' basket. If a colonising power can replace an indigenous belief system then you can create your own spiritual sanctuary and inner temple. Sadly, as I said at the beginning, people often find their faith only at the end, when they cling to hope because of imminent death.

Within the tribe you collect for yourself is your spiritual identity. Trusting in something outside your physical identity is the beginning of finding your spiritual tools. How you choose to create your temple is up to you. Understanding that spirituality is a self-care tool is the message I want to deliver, and all you need to do is identify what things you already have in place and what things you may now consider would complement your basket of wellness tools.

Meditation

All the darkness in the world can't put out the light of one candle.

Confucius.

Throughout the text I have mentioned that I use meditation as my go-to place when I need to rebalance myself. I have also introduced the term mindfulness practice. Now I want to expand on both practices to explain how they are different, and also to show my respect to Buddhist, Hindu and Zen disciplines. These teachings in mindfulness understanding have been shared with the Western World, in a simplified format. Sadly it seems to be diluted from the essence and wholeness of the learning that defined the path of student and the dedication it took to reach master-level status.

Meditation for me is a devout practice that brings me to divinity. Some would say this is God, which is true, but it also brings me close to conversations across the spirit realm. This practice has developed my sentient, audio and vision abilities, which have helped me in appreciating my clairvoyant and healing resources.

Meditation practice is a welcome ritual that nurtures and nourishes my biological, psychological, social and spiritual aspects of self. I began my journey with transcendental meditation, which was a twenty-minute sitting meditation focusing on my breathing. I did this for six months struggling to find nirvana. I eventually stopped the practice for two years. I returned to the practice to appreciate the healing of the stillness within. The moments of nirvana came often, and continue to come. Nirvana is many things and nothing, being content and insightful within nothingness. It is not one type of destination. Nirvana is love within that radiates out because this is the knowingness of being within the 'I am' – which is your soul, your temple. Being in human love interrupts your senses and lightens your perceptions. Nirvana does the same, but the focal point is nothingness and expansion, which is inner peace and inner self-love.

The healing and calming benefits of meditation have been renamed into mindfulness practice to remove the esoteric and divinity stigma, making the practice mainstreamed and thus commercially acceptable. Mindfulness focuses on the breath and attitude, so you attain inner calm, intention and gratitude. I feel that mindfulness is opening the door to meditation without the ritualistic dedication to the practice. Mindfulness practice is comfortable, whereas types of meditation can be physically or psychologically uncomfortable for some people.

I believe mindfulness is what is experienced before the dedication to a meditation practice is routinely established. Mindfulness practice is simple to incorporate as a wellness tool to help alleviate stress, find calm, and find focus.

Brahmacharya

Life is a balance between holding on and letting go.

Rumi.

Our journey through the exploration of how personal energy fields overlap with other people brings us to ponder the unified sexual energy interplay between established lovers, or short-term sexual partners.

Earlier we discussed how some orgasm experiences may transcend the physical sexual act and reach towards spiritual ascension, generating a higher vibration frequency, or simply a sustained all-body orgasm. We also mentioned that your body is your temple, and that temples are a place of reverence.

This being said, when you are sharing your body with another you are sharing in their energy, and they are sharing yours. Sexual sharing sometimes turns into sexual regret — those interludes that looked great through the lens of alcohol, urge and easiness. The morning after tells a different story — one of regret and shame. This is acted out as escape and hide, and managed by ignoring the text messages and blocking social media so that hopefully you can forget this ever happened.

Your energy is your personal bubble; it acts like your fingerprint, and it's your language. When you share your bubble with a lover you are sharing your fingerprint and language, just as they share their energy bubble, fingerprint and language with you.

Energy transference is much like a sexually transmitted disease (STD). Dis-ease being the focus here. How, you may ask, is this possible? Think of energy as being personal vitality. When you share your body with an energy-depleted person they share in your energy — they bathe in your energy at its pure essence. They consume your energy to feel good, but they don't leave an equal sharing of vitality. They leave, the sex was great, but you're feeling drained. Keep repeating this cycle and you compromise your immune system. When sexual union is balanced in vital energy, then both parties have equity in energy sharing.

Look to the pattern that is generated if you habitually have multiple partners or if you are in a long-term union with an energy-deficient lover. You are losing vitality.

When a relationship ends and the lovers take their loving elsewhere within a short timeframe, they essentially still have the energy residue of the past lover in their field. This crossover is much like the perfume that is left on clothing long after the last spray. Essentially if both lovers hook-up quickly with new people, they still hold the energy of their past lover. If the new partners are also newly split, in effect two new lovers coupling can collectively carry the crossover energy of multiple lovers. This energy orgy depletes personal vitality. It is sharing dirty bathwater, and it does not respect your temple or your current lover's temple.

Brahmacharya is one of the five restraints or yamas in yogic teaching. Essentially it is about abstinence or control of sexual activity. The focus here is shared sexual pleasure, but it can be extended to include self-pleasure if that is compulsive. Brahmacharya acknowledges that sexual energy and spiritual energy are unified and that they should be in harmony with each other, so you need to be wise with how you use this energy.

Cleaning up sexual habits for a better sexual quality and energy frequency is much like Tantric teaching, which is considered the catalyst for higher consciousness sexual and spiritual transformation.

Eastern energy philosophy states that you can become ill by burning your Qi, which is vital energy. Jing is the body and all its functions, which begin to suffer from depleted Qi energy. Western medicine says the aging process reduces testosterone production and reserves, and ejaculation uses testosterone reserves. This is like gifting $10 notes to everyone, not realising that the financial reserve is capped at a point. Where your self-care heads in terms of this energy exchange within your love-making ritual is personal. The sacredness of your body temple and your enduring vitality needs exploration to bring into question if your practice is respectful and sustainable.

Drama Hook

Love conquers all things; let us surrender to love.

Virgil.

Once you realise you need to take off the cloak of a finished relationship there is usually some drama to process, creating personal energy depletion.

Within most interpersonal relationship dynamics, when things go south bad energy is created and can be fed continuously with action and reaction interplays. Managing reaction to drama is a personal choice, and part of self-care.

From the perspective of health and wellbeing it is advantageous to monitor your invested energy in finding respectful distance, quiet resolution or closure, depending on the desired outcome.

However within conflict situations you can become embroiled in ceaseless drama upon drama. Why? Because the language used will be blaming, accusing, insulting, insinuating, bullying, denying, lying and designed to hurt in order to get a reaction. There are at least two actors who are in conflict, and then bystanders fuelling the conflict in support of one particular actor, or trying to mediate. Then there are the observers sharing their thoughts. This all creates negative energy.

Negative energy radiates from both inner and outer conflict. Outer conflict involves space, values, possessions and people. Inner conflict is personal turmoil, which sometimes has no voice, and can be the place of quiet drama hooks, or possibly self-persecution, denial, fear and silence. It is here that the earlier mentioned co-dependency pattern within relationships will thrive in the atmosphere of intensified drama creation.

The drama hook is the piece of the personality that is governed by ego and that needs to retract from, or react to the conflict or crisis situation. It is a hook because it catches onto the drama and is determined to be the innocent actor in the real-life play. Identifying your drama hook history will help identify your action and reaction defence game plan and recognise your own programme of play and hooks.

Why do people waste time trying to win an emotional battle? How many battles have you invested your energy in, losing your balance, your joy, your time? Is the drama worth the energy output? Emotional wars are never won; everyone gets a map of anger and disappointment to orientate the battleground of loss, hurt, frustration and confusion.

We have the right to choose not to play the antagonist/protagonist game. We can use neutral words and ask for 'time out'; we can ask for distance. We can request that we are left out of the drama loop. We can choose to see only the good aspect of the situation. We can choose how to invest our energy, just like we choose to stay in the drama. We can also be discerning about which dispute requires personal involvement, since there are times when you will need to be confrontational. Some individuals may need the help of a counsellor to find inner resources that will help them challenge their inner confliction that can hold them perplexed within drama situations.

This is a reality shifter. You can choose your perspective and reaction in any unfolding drama. Drama requires players, and the drama game is like a fire — it loses momentum if there is no source of fuel for the fire. Mindfulness skills such as calm breathing, neutral language and well-thought-out actions develop a framework of respectful observation and assessment. Drama needs 'thinking space', and thinking can become compulsive. Compulsive thoughts drain vital energy, depleting energy reserves and creating inner stress. Choosing to minimise how you invest in drama is your choice of how you 'spend' your vitality. Vitality is not an endless reservoir of endless energy; it comes at a cost to your long-term health and wellbeing.

An example of drama and conflicted viewpoints is the classic grubby teenage bedroom. The parent wants the room clean, while the teenager likes it dark and dirty. The parent owns the teenager and the bedroom, and has house rules. The teenager wants autonomy, food, clothes, money, and their personal, grubby, dark space to chill in. Both players are functioning from Ego and resistance. Resistance uses vital energy.

Mindfulness practice can be utilised by both invested parties, but it doesn't adjust the situation. Both parent and teenager can be breathing through the conflict challenge of 'clean your room' versus 'this is my room and you don't have jurisdiction in here' debates. Sometimes differing perspectives challenge any resolution because few people think about the supposed antagonist's view in the conflict situation.

Critical reflection is a skill used in conflict resolution; this means taking a moment to try to understand all of the stakeholder's perspectives within the conflict. Some people don't like to validate the opponent's argument since it weakens the reasoning of the conflict. Putting some distance between individual debates lessens the immediate drama of the situation. This time out can help people find perspective and think about how to negotiate a better outcome for all parties involved.

Critical reflection is developed at the individual level. Changing a reaction-and-action programme that was modelled through a life of influence is your choice. Removing yourself from drama situations is demonstrating your human right to feel safe. Choosing to maintain self-regulation and self-respect is often the way forward to managing yourself, as well as your personal energy within conflict.

Let's go back to the example offered with the grubby teenager's bedroom and the parent wanting a clean bedroom. There are so many reasons justifying each stakeholder's needs and wants that it's futile to waste everyone's time. The answer is to discern the difference between what's really important, what's averagely important, and what's not very important in your perspective.

What's the reality shifter? If the child died unexpectedly you would live knowing you wasted time on the tidy-room-drama — and now you would give anything to have a living child with a dirty bedroom…

The most important aspect is personal health and wellbeing. Intentional negativity with thoughts, actions and speech is self-harming. Drama addiction is a self-perpetuating, ongoing drainage of vital energy. You choose how you spend your vital energy just as much as you choose how to expel personal pollution and manufacture your vital energy.

Sleep

Those who lose dreaming are lost.

Aboriginal Proverb.

Sleep is the place of mind and body restoration. It is governed by the hormone melatonin, which is mostly secreted from the pineal gland in the brain. Melatonin's job is the repetitive biological cycle of: induce sleep, sleep soundly, dream and wake up. This is the circadian rhythm. Good sleep is a vital self-care activity that restores adrenal function, mental functioning and memory recall, and stimulates tissue, muscle and bone regeneration. Good sleep patterns provide renewed vitality and a positive outlook. Poor sleep patterns contribute to anxiety, depression, fatigue, irritability, reduced immunity, and a lack of concentration to name just a few hazards of sleep deprivation.

However sleep is more than a biological, physiological and psychological necessity. It is the place of dreaming. Dreaming is a way of 'knowing', 'seeing' and 'astral travelling' for indigenous cultures and subcultures the world over. Researchers struggle to understand this type of sensing because it is individually, culturally, and historically subjective.

Research has provided information on all aspects of sleep processes to accurately diagnose and help people experiencing sleep dysphoria. Sleep has two basic brain states, being Rapid Eye Movement (REM), which is when most of the dreaming happens, and Non-Rem (NREM) which is the place of deep, restorative sleep. Sleep depth and the pattern of moving in and out of REM and NREM sleep varies over any given night's sleep, going from NREM through to mostly REM. That is why dream recall is memorable on waking up.

Sigmund Freud and Carl Jung, early psychoanalysts, believed that dreams are the window into the inner thoughts of people, and that dream interpretation could unravel the essence of their concern. Indigenous and Shaman practice supports the idea that dream information can deliver guidance of births or deaths, visitations and news from the spirit world.

Poor sleep, nightmares, and fear and anxiety responses can affect our sleep psychology.

Sleep paralysis is a condition where the person wakes in fear of being strangled, being intruded upon by some entity or flying, creating a fight/flight response. This is thought to be a dysfunction or fragmentation within the REM sleep and waking stages. The remedy is varied, incorporating sleep routines, sleeping tablets and antidepressants. Sometimes a person has created a sleep pattern out of anxiety of not being able to sleep; therefore the sleep belief becomes dominant over attempting to change the routine. This can be addressed with intervention like cognitive behavioural therapy.

Brain waves are electrical messages that can be measured with EEG instruments. Brain-wave activity presents in bands: Beta (awake);

Alpha (eyes closed, daydreaming); Theta (drowsiness and light sleep); Delta (deep sleep). REM sleep is comprised of Alpha and Theta waves. NREM is Delta waves.

Theta waves are the place of light sleep, but also the place where meditators dwell without going to sleep. This is interesting because it is also REM sleep, the place of dreaming. Insight comes to many people from dreaming and meditative states. Thus when we go back to view sleep-paralysis symptoms of entity visitation and flying experience could this also link to indigenous and spiritualist practice of receiving insight. It is subjective, but it could be as simple as being fearful of REM sleep experiences.

From my personal experience of dreaming I have at times been given information, protection and guidance to keep me and my family safe. I have met my unborn babies in utero. I have been forewarned of my people dying. I have bought great houses. I have met people in dream state before the physical meeting. I have flown astral to see what was needed to know. Early on I met negative energies, and yes, I was scared; I learnt that they can be easily removed with intentional protection of God affirmation or prayer. From my understanding, Ascension — which is enlightenment — is the journey towards Heaven, and at each level of intuitive skill development is a testing ground marked with fears to be overcome before you move up a level towards Graceful Surrender.

Who looks outside dreams; who looks inside, awakes.

Carl Jung.

Therefore I believe that my dreaming has been an amazing teacher of things not visioned until they are dreamed and proved into existence. I learnt to trust my dreams, and consequently I think Freudian and Jungian beliefs about dreams being a window to the inner life are correct. But they are also a field trip into the future, and sleep is just one of the pathways you can go down to develop this type of guidance…

Section Four - Part 2

Your Wellbeing, Your Way

Self-Care Starts With You

You are the controller of your life moving forward. This last section introduces some tools that may be of help for you along the way to manifest wellness, belonging, healing and self-regulation.

I offer a short list of tools that can be added to a wellness plan. I urge you to formulate your own list of therapeutic tools that benefit you directly. Only you know what you're feeling and thinking. And only you know when your balance is wobbly.

It is good to view your self-care as a prescription that enhances your overall biological, psychological, social and spiritual balance.

Your body is with you for life; it is your temple. Respect it with nutrient-rich food and clean water, and protect it from environmental abuse. Exercise it often. Care for it like you would a loved friend. Your body is not separate from your mind. But people tend to honour the mind while disrespecting the importance of their body until it starts to break down in its functioning. This ignorance shows up in dis-ease, which really is a body not at ease — not in a state of homeostasis.

There will always be conditions within the body and mind outside of the simplistic self-care of our health, but if you factor in personal health ownership and a health management plan before functioning diminishes with age or illness you may avert conditions or prolong their onset, and maybe re-correct health at the cellular level.

Nutrient and Medication

Having an understanding of nutrient support to aid the mind and body is important for the replicating of cells, and the management of stress. Our diets are varied, and sometimes circumstances lead us to poor nutrition. Stress burns up reserves of vitamins and nutrients that help regulate balance. Visiting a health shop and asking for nutrient support to cope with stress or any symptoms you display is honouring your body and mind. Establishing a relationship with the nutrient professional is another tool in self-care management.

There are many books on healthy eating and symptoms of nutrient deficiency with explanations pertaining to the health benefits of every vitamin and mineral supplement. When the body is under stress it easily burns up its reserves of available nutrient stores and this is why it's sometimes necessary to take supplements. Prolonged deficiency can lead to slow wound healing, agitation, stress, anxiety and depression, and if left unchecked can progress to fatigue reactions. The Google search and health blog avenues are readily available and instant tools to streamline your understanding of symptoms and possible nutrient concerns.

All general practitioners are health professional 'tools' who can diagnose your symptoms and refer you for a variety of tests including comprehensive blood and allergy tests to detect any deficiency, irritant, or dis-ease. Many pharmaceutical or prescribed medicines are anti-nutrient. They can deplete existing reserves, or reduce absorption of vitamins and minerals vital for healthy immune function. Ask your GP for relative or absolute contraindications regarding any drugs and procedures. (And do your own Google search).

Becoming active in your health research increases your confidence when discussing your observations and concerns about your health care. You are the promoter of your own health destiny and you can make good choices when you are informed. Being proactive means you are a partner in your health-care plan, and you will become confident at asking why a pharmaceutical medication or surgery is suggested. Ask for a full explanation as to how the health professional came to that diagnosis/plan. Ask about alternative treatment options, if any, and ask for a second opinion. Here you become the wellness tool.

Exercise

There is no denying that exercise has positive benefit to physical and psychological wellbeing. The health benefits outweigh wasted time with procrastination.

Exercise can be a fun way to rejuvenate the body and mind. It is known to improve mood, increase self-esteem, reduce anxiety and lift depression, which in turn helps us manage our stress levels. Exercise helps us sleep better, which contributes to managing mood and improving immune function. When you improve muscle tone and flexibility, you strengthen heart, lung and circulation performance. Overall strength training can improve health and lift self-esteem.

When the body is being exercised it can induce elation with the release of endorphins, which are natural opiates. Vigorous exercise induces euphoria which is an instant mood lifter and de-stressor, and can instil a state of inner emotional calm. So exercise promotes a healthy body and mind. It also is mostly inclusive and social. Exercise inspires people to set health and fitness plans. Control is required since over-exercising can create body stress and injury.

Exercise in any form assists structural, biochemical and psychological wellness; therefore it is a tool to add to a wellness plan.

Yoga, Tai Chi, Qigong, Dance and Breath

Surrendering your soul to the practice of yoga, tai chi, qigong, or dance is a continuation of exercise practice. These disciplines cross into mindfulness practice, strengthening the physical body while developing dynamic breathwork, which relaxes both mind and body.

Breathwork originates in the Eastern disciplines of health management. The practice focuses on conscious attention to both the inhaling and exhaling of breath. The breathing techniques are extended with yogic breathing, referred to as Pranayama, being the source of our prana or vital life force.

Breathwork is beneficial to managing anxiety symptoms by slowing and regulating the breath across the inhale and exhale. Anxiety is brought on by the mind feeling threat. The body tenses, the heart races, the endocrine system pumps out stress hormones aiding a potential stress and anxiety reaction, to the initial feeling of threat or danger.

The conscious management of deep, balanced, slow breathing sends a comforting message to your brain and autonomic nervous system, assuring them that your fear is manageable and your body and mind are now feeling safe.

These disciplines allow an individual to explore alternative movement and exercise options. Each discipline is a wellness tool since they promote personal vitality with expressive movement.

Levels of Touch

Comforting touch is a human need. It may be in the context of structural alignment or mending of physiological breaks, sprains or maladjustment. It could also be therapeutic or somatic touch, relieving strain and relaxing the soft tissues of the body. There is the body work of reiki and touch therapy, as well as the meridian energy work of traditional Chinese medicine.

Each modality works to their theoretical or philosophical perspective and speciality. The physical body modalities work with musculoskeletal function and structure to correct posture, locate maladaptive patterns and correct function. Massage therapy can relieve stress-induced aches, move lymphatic fluid, and release toxic by-products. Off-the-body energy work can align energy fields, creating physical grounding and the restoration of inner balance caused by shock.

Some people are very uncomfortable with being touched, either physically or emotionally. Trusting another person to see and touch your body can be traumatic. The denial of touch and abuse of touch is not an unusual experience within some families. Therefore it can't be assumed that everybody is comfortable with being touched.

Yet touch is something we all desire. Many people allow the concept of sexual intimacy to be their touch vehicle. This is limiting the joy of sharing our bodies to just being support for another human. Non-sexual touching of hands, heads, and legs can simply relax someone, reaffirming that physical gesture can support in times of joy, sadness, celebration and grieving.

Sharing hugs is a cathartic exploration of connection, welcome, trust, care, support and respect, whether the recipient/partner is a single person, group, an animal, a soft toy or a tree. This type of touch can be learned… become comfortable to accept this type of supportive touch. I learnt to accept hugs in my early adulthood. I faked hugs until I began to enjoy the sharing of energy within the hug dynamic.

Not all people need touch and it is our responsibility to assess the person's body language prior to initiating physical touch and hugs. If a person squirms, pulls away or says, 'I don't want to be touched', *listen and respect* their boundaries. Also respect cultural difference with physical touch.

A person may have been violated or abused, and automatically is hypervigilant to protect themselves from being touched. Touch becomes a trust issue and needs time and empathetic understanding as well as therapeutic intervention from suitably qualified people.

However most people enjoy soft-tissue therapy to reduce muscular tension, and rejuvenating spa treatments are designed for total relaxation. Everyone who mends an injury cherishes reducing physical pain and gaining mobility. Therefore medical, structural and therapeutic touch is beneficial as a health and empowerment tool. Physical touch is a tool of healing and care when it is welcomed, professional, and feels safe for all parties. Being mindful of equity and boundary rules is paramount to safe touch exchange.

Talk Therapy

It is sometimes easier to take medication for numbing than confront thinking. There are times when exploration around behaviour or reactions needs to be opened up and discussed. It is only when we speak that we hear ourselves. Talk therapy gives us that vehicle to hear our internal self-talk and unpack our thinking. Internal dialogue can blindside our ability to get clarity or direction because we seem to recycle thoughts without resolving them. Hearing ourselves audibly puts another dimension to our choice of language, tone and focus.

Psychological wellbeing is sometimes stunted for many years due to traumatic experience. It can affect how we interact with our world and result in behaviour and thinking that does not mirror our authentic inner self. This maladjusted self-projection often felt by the person can lead to maladaptive personal belief, and manifest itself in further skewed behaviour.

There are many options of talk therapy. Counsellors offer a broad set of skills, while psychotherapy builds on counselling skills through exploring movement, roleplaying, and writing depending on therapist preference. Self-help groups with a central theme offer group belonging, and on-topic support. Websites offer information pathways. Indigenous therapists, church groups and clairvoyant mediums can offer clarity and sense. Begin with a Google search around the varied talk therapies on offer in your region.

Of course anyone can help another person by hearing them. There will always be wise souls who become empathetic and helpful just by living life. Many life-changing stories have come about because of the advice or empathy of a stranger. Wisdom comes when you least expect it. But sometimes you have to go hunt it down.

Becoming comfortable to reach for therapy before you hit repetitive rock bottoms is the aim of learning to value talk therapy as a coping and direction wellness tool. Unfortunately many people have to be very hurt before they share their vulnerability with others.

The saying *'hurt people, hurt people'* emphasises how the roll-on effect of a disarranged person's action or inaction can damage the people surrounding them. This is a good reason to explore any antagonistic reactive behaviour that doesn't serve you authentically. Talk therapy is a vehicle for self-change and understanding.

There are various forums that offer group, family or individual therapy that will be on-topic and create a confidential, safe community of listeners and facilitators. They will cover addiction behaviour, domestic violence, sexual assault and marriage counselling, to name a few. Each group will have extensive understanding and information networks for further help, as will one-on-one counselling sessions.

All you need to do is become comfortable with the idea that sharing your concern is cathartic. Realise there are people who will help you reframe perspectives in your understanding and life choices at every intersection along the way.

Autobiographical Influence

Other people's life stories can be motivational reality shifters. Reading autobiographies or watching movies or documentaries that recount other people's crises and turning points can add perspective to your own crisis story. These mediums share the strengths and resources that helped survivors through their experience, and these may be inspirational and life-changing in your own story.

Volunteer

The best way to find yourself is to lose yourself in the service of others.

Mahatma Gandhi.

Give and take is the balance of life. By breathing in oxygen and expelling carbon dioxide you are volunteering to save the trees, just as the trees breathe in the carbon dioxide and expel the oxygen, volunteering to save your life. Everyone has purpose and value to benefit another. You are volunteering to share a breath, a smile, a hug, a shoulder to cry on. Volunteer when you see a need. Action the sign asking for help.

Volunteering your skills and time extends your social networks into communities you might never have got the opportunity to be part of. It allows you to share a smile or an appreciative moment. Volunteering your abilities opens the door into another community tribe, and may expand your skillset along with your worldview.

Nature and Animals

Nature never did betray the heart that loved her.

William Wordsworth.

When we think of nature it resonates through all our senses. We all have a memory of being lost in the moment, gazing at a watercourse or stand of trees, or maybe a meadow where bees flitted effortlessly from flower to flower simply going about their day. Or ocean waves may have consumed taking hold of our gaze in an abstract pattern of simplicity and power. Nature is one of the most complete healing tools when you are willingly immersed in it. Some liken it to being within their inner temple, the place of contemplation, cleansing the rebalancing of emotions and the grounding of scattered energy.

It is apt to place the intrinsic appeal of the natural world as a personal balance tool for centring yourself. Yet not everyone has access to big expanses of the natural environment to find solace. In days gone by, before the industrial revolution, we were all connected to small provinces and kinship networks that depended on the land and celebrated with seasonal rituals. This affinity to the natural world stems from our reliance on it to sustain and support survival.

Today our society connects food availability to a supermarket. We are so far removed from our earth and water connections. Our circadian clock is attuned to a screen, not the rhythm and cycle of nature. Many people live in apartments, walk on concrete paths, smell smog, and drink bottled water. They might find a small park to sit in a green patch near a manmade pond among a few trees.

There are cultures removed from their ancestral lands and community. These disenfranchised people who no longer have their land connection find their sense of mental wellbeing is affected. Urban communities may provide green spaces but any indigenous person is subliminally disenfranchised until they touch their own ground again.

There is a spiritual connection to the place where your ancestors are buried. There is also a spiritual connection to the natural world. This is why people should value the healing and balance gained from spending time with nature.

The natural world delights our five main senses of sight, hearing, smell, taste and touch, and the sixth sense of inner knowing. Creating a Zen space or display in your home that is filled with images of nature, plants, water features or tactile interactive natural things you've collected can be a simple nature solace tool.

Visiting the natural world can be through the companionship and healing of animals. Caring for an animal makes you share yourself. An animal can be a confidante, a non-judgemental friend, something to stroke and be touched by, and to share love with. Pets can create conversation with others and a thread to other friendships.

Strangers will greet an animal before they will greet another person. Animals offer us strength when all else is failing around us, much as hugging a tree can support us when our world is imploding and we need something solid to cling to. The natural world is an important part of your collection of wellness tools, just like a valued member of the tribe that you need to collect around you for balance.

Complementary Therapies

Within the healing and wellness realm there are diverse therapies on offer — too many to mention here. People who gravitate towards alternative health options can often find great help. Some are conservative and sceptical about trusting themselves, let alone a therapy that is not backed up by medical research.

If you undertake a Google search of complementary therapies, a range of options are presented. In the West we are comfortable with a mainstream medical model that assesses presenting symptoms of discomfort or dis-ease. Complementary therapies blow open options within assessment to incorporate the whole person, including symptoms. Traditional Chinese medicine and Indian ayurveda medicine are two of the oldest approaches working from this mindset. Complementary therapy will incorporate your spirituality, as will indigenous health assessment and treatment tools.

Homeopathy, Bach flower remedies, Aura-Soma Essences, Western and Chinese herbalism, and aromatherapy are some of the complementary therapy doors waiting to be opened. Life is an adventure when you embrace new knowledge. It is recommended that you be your own pioneer with your health and wellness exploration. Sadly many people get adventurous when they are diagnosed with a complicated illness, and even then some will take the medical opinion as gospel.

Integrated therapy is something medical professionals are welcoming in their quest to help patients. Many medically trained professionals are incorporating complementary therapy suggestions in their consultations with clients. This is a new trend that honours the need of the patient.

Self-Belief

Self-belief is the motivator that creates opportunity, but can also be the negator of opportunity. At this point I want you to understand that how you think can be a very powerful self-care tool.

Some readers will struggle with the idea that faith and the conviction of your thoughts can change your outlook and create positive outcomes and experiences. Others will already have an understanding that "what you think about, you bring about". This transpires across both positive and negative attention on events, opportunities and entitlement.

Thoughts are intentional projections that can manifest oppressive circumstances or abundance. If you want more detail and explanation around the concept of abundance read *The Secret* or watch the movie by Rhonda Bryne.

Most people are stuck in their past memory of pivotal events. Over time the memory becomes distorted and biased, yet people base their thinking on their perspective of events.

Paying conscious attention to your thoughts is the beginning of mastering them. The concept of experiencing life from "a cup half full" or "a cup half empty" is a simple analogy. People react differently to the same scenario — some see demise while others see opportunity.

If you want to become conscious of your thinking to create a positive change in your reaction to events, the first thing you need to do is learn to control your allocated time to a negative thought. You can think about it fleetingly, but let it go quickly since it holds you in a deficit ledger. If something positive happens think about it for longer and say thank you to yourself because this thinking holds you in a positive ledger. The objective is to build abundant positive thoughts.

It is hard to control your thinking when bad things happen, but by becoming aware of your dominant thinking style you can learn to master it. We all fall off the wagon of positivity and lose our footing. The game is to find some tools to help move you back to a positive perspective.

Losing your footing on thoughts is like being lost in a big city. It gets scary but it's easy to navigate if you have a Google app that can bring up a map to help.

Do a Google search of positive affirmations about happiness, health, money, love, fun and laughter. Keep a collection of jokes, watch funny movies, and help someone else out of a bind.

Activity:

Spend time doing something enjoyable with your tribe. Create your mantra of happiness and abundance.

Self-Love

You can search throughout the entire universe for someone who is more deserving of your love and affection than you are yourself, and that person is not to be found anywhere. You yourself, as much as anybody in the entire universe deserve your love and affection.

Siddhartha Gautama Buddha.

Self-love is the relationship you form with yourself and is integral to your foundation of how you love others. To say that you focus your attention on building personal self-love may seem egotistical or arrogant. Our society doesn't encourage this notion. Yet the scriptures put equal value on self-love when they state 'love your neighbour as you love yourself'.

Society encourages kindness and love going out into the universe to others. Yet this practice depletes an individual if they don't have skills of generating love for themselves. Many people enter relationships to find love, investing love onto their partner, but this love depletes their reserve over time as the romantic euphoria diminishes. An individual becomes 'needy' for the love from the other partner. This love may be less than expected, or redundant of reciprocal love. The message is that to give love to another, you must have love to give. Therefore you need to prioritise manufacturing enough love to share.

Unconditional love is giving and receiving love without conditions placed on the recipients. Unconditional love should be the love you give yourself as your wellness tool. When you are in a commercial airliner the air stewards walk you through the oxygen mask routine, stipulating that you must put the mask on yourself first before you help others with theirs. Why? Because you may well end up being dead if you give your care and love to others before you care for yourself.

Self-love is self-care; the implementing and prioritising of self-care tools is the beginning of building self-love rituals. Self-love is remembering that the love you hold for yourself is pure and unconditional respect for yourself.

Many disarranged people have low self-worth because the love afforded them was tainted with a confusing game played out over their early life, and they have carried this confusion into later relationships. Cry now for the pain that followed you through your life because the love never came… now you change the rules of love, you choose to love yourself first.

Shut your eyes, fall in love, stay there

Rumi.

How do you manufacture your love? You find joy, you live joy, you sprinkle joy on everything, and you shower in joy every waking hour. It is enough being you. You give love to the flowers, you give love to the grass, and nature gives love back, you listen to beautiful music. You read beautiful mantras. You say 'I love you' to your image in the mirror each day since this may be the only love you hear given to you. If you practise this, one day you'll start effortlessly telling others you love them.

Cultivating your garden of love requires nurture and regular attention. In your life you may have yearned for this pure love that never came the way you needed it, and chances are it never will arrive the way you need it. So only you know how you need love. Think about those times that you needed love from others.

Activity:

Write a sentence describing the type of love you needed to hear, whether it be forgiveness love, thankful love, appreciation love, apologetic love, acceptance love, or simply 'I love you' love. Now you have identified things you needed to hear. Make these sentences come to life by reading them to yourself as healing mantra. What you never had from these people or what wasn't delivered the way you needed it can come to completion with this exercise.

The last thing to do is forgive the wrongs, forgive the memories, forgive the times you were hurt by actions you didn't order for yourself. Go back to the Speed Bump Personal Template (Pg 12) and look in the end column titled… Your Feelings Now. These feelings hold you stuck.

It's time to release them.

Activity:

Visualise a gold-coloured helium-filled balloon.

Write on the balloon one of the feelings identified in the column.

Release the balloon into the atmosphere. Watch it leave you. Feel the lightness and peace fill the space within you that was stuck because of the holding onto that feeling.

Say goodbye, thank it for going on its way now, forgive it for confusing you, and watch it float away.

Repeat this exercise with all the feelings you have noted in this column.

You can choose to do this activity with real helium-filled balloons, a marker pen, and a space that feels good for this forgiveness exercise.

You need to know you are loved, and that you are special, that the essence of you is beautiful, valuable love. Practicing self-love as self-care is the most gracious and respectful gifting of inspiration that you can give the people you share space with.

This is your moment to optimise your thinking about how you can enhance your life by practising an attitude of gratitude. Recap the great things that happened to you, for you, around you today and each day that you are blessed to breathe on this wonderful planet that you share with a multitude of people who experience a mixed bag of disappointment and opportunity. Lighten the collective energy of your world by choosing to model positive interactions with all humanity. And learn to love the jigsaw puzzle of your unique life.

Be grateful every day.

Namaste

"My soul honours your soul. I honour the place in you where the entire universe resides. I honour the light, love, truth, beauty & peace within you, because it is also within me. In sharing these things we are united, we are the same, we are one."

Hindu Welcome.

Epilogue

Ko Wai Au? Who Am I?

Ko wai au is the New Zealand Māori term that inspired this writing. 'Who am I?' should be an easy question to answer, yet I struggled with this question. The answer is evasive because I know parts of myself. I know facets of me enough to get by. I know how to dream and aspire for today and the future. I understand yesterday and the preceding yesterdays based on my interpretation of my memories. I know I bumped and bounced through my life to this point, much like being in a carnival bumper car. All the cars I bumped into or got bumped by represent the people or structures that pushed, moulded, manoeuvred, shunted, nudged, guided, corrected, forced, bullied, suggested, directed, influenced, aligned and nurtured my journey on this long road trip.

Who am I? as a concept remains incomplete, but through the writing of *Locate Yourself* I can articulate more of who I am and explain why I think I am who I think I am. Yet I am aware that I am a thousand-piece jigsaw puzzle with a component of my identity missing, and those missing pieces hold the vital essence of a ko wai au legacy I live in wonder of.

As a child I remember being incredibly envious of the families on my street because they seemed to have many aunties, uncles and cousins. I was envious of their family connections. My adopted family was small, and geographic distance meant our family connections were limited to the names of people we rarely saw. Also my adopted father was an antisocial person, preferring to keep people on the other side of the fence.

Who am I? - A product of all the previous stuff.

My 'stuff' of connection showed itself in my teenage years. Some would say it was the spirit realm making themselves active as protectors and guides. The guidance was a different kind of bumper car — etheric, and not of my family culture. I have since learned that the spirit realm is a language. As with all languages, you need to learn individual words before you can understand the flow of the terminology.

Spirit language is received across our senses as messages. The communication can be felt, heard, smelt, tasted, dreamed, guided or intuitively sensed; it could be delivered in signs, and instrumented with tools. It can be a complicated language to interpret and trust. This is subjective, but I offer a brief explanation of the passing process:

Purposeful Communications

When the body dies, the soul is released back to the 'other side' or the 'afterlife', which is known as the spirit realm. Within this realm it is the soul's purpose to evaluate the life lived and the lessons learned. The crossover from human living to spirit living is the juncture of evaluation. There are some souls that stay in limbo in this world by choice or due to lack of direction through the void. Reincarnation is the process of choosing to be reborn to continue the journey of ascension learning if that is required. To be reincarnated is personal choice and alignment of new family, culture and geography providing the continuation of the purpose of attaining this 'life time' learning. The transition journey back to this world is free choice; the purpose of these journeys through time is to become enlightened in thoughts and actions. People who die with an understanding or belief of the possibility of heaven or spirit-realm communication will find it much easier and quicker to find a way to communicate with their loved ones in this living world. They will also know the open channel within the family members to focus on to get a message through. The spirits want to deliver the message that they are okay, that life is good on the 'other side', that they are hanging out with passed-over family, and that they are well and living without pain. They also like to apologise for any pain they caused. They do this to comfort the living in times of grieving, and to demonstrate that death is another doorway to our soul's evolution to the angelic realm, which sits above the spirit realm. The angelic realm is attained after the repetitive journeys through the reincarnation process of ascension and enlightenment.

Spirit communication has been a welcome connection with my deceased parents. They rally around me to protect me. They are noticeable with their spirit signatures, which alert me to their presence. It is important to realise that the apology from the spirit realm is pure and comforting. The spirits see how their actions and inactions caused pain or confusion. It is here that I must mention that my deceased mother was supportive in making this writing come alive. In her living world she knew that I was intuitively open. Not long after her death she visited early one morning to tell me she had made it through the void and she told me her story and intention. My adopted mother in death is still actively supporting me. This is an important aspect to 'Who am I?' since I do a disservice to myself and my spirit guidance if I don't honour their efforts to deliver apologies and confirm their soul existence.

Yet there is a mystery to me with the Māori ancestral spirit realm that comes to me — a mystery of why they present with teachings of ko wai au. There is a rumour that my biological father was a part-Māori policeman from over the back fence in Manurewa, a suburb of Auckland, New Zealand. I believe this might be why guidance comes from them; I seem to see into the Māori spirit world. The spirits hold me in Northland — they say I'm from here. This is the last mystery to solve for my standing place in this lifetime. And if I'm not of Māori descent, however diluted, my belief is that Māori tupuna saw a child yearning for blood connection to the whenua, and graciously shared in their resources and their ways, weaving their story into my story. This is the legacy I hand on to my children, explaining ko wai au.

Thank you.

Acknowledgments

This work is an evolution of my learning over my life course thus far. Therefore it is not the work of one person. The teachers and healers are many.

I would sincerely like to thank all the people and books who entered and exited my life over this time.

I thank Elsa Jayne Lydia and John George for adopting me. I thank my siblings for giving me connection, purpose and memories. I thank my family for the love we share. I thank my friends who encouraged me. I thank my daughters: River for technical support and Harna for graphics. I thank Ella, Lauren and Grant for critiquing, Lesley Marshall for editing and Stacey Milich for cover photography. I needed all of your help to craft Locate Yourself.

Further Reading

Addis, Michael E., Invisible Men, Times Books, 2011.

Bays, Brandon, The Journey, Harper Element, 2012.

Beattie, Melody, Codependent No More, Collins Dove, 1989.

Beckett, Chris, Assessment & Intervention in Social Work, Sage Publications Ltd, 2010.

Biddulph, Steve, Manhood, Finch Publishing, 2002.

Brownstein, Art, Extraordinary Healing, Harbor Press, 2005.

Byrne, Rhonda, The Secret, Atria Books, 2006.

Chopra, Deepak, Reinventing the Body, Resurrecting the Soul, Rider, 2009.

Dale, Cyndi, The Subtle Body: An Encyclopedia of Your Energetic Anatomy, Sounds True, 2009.

Forward, Susan, Toxic Parents, Bantam Books, 2002.

Freire, Paulo, Pedagogy of the Oppressed, Penguin Books, 1996.

Fry, Colin, Secrets of the Afterlife, Rider-Ebury Publishing, 2008

Kapleau, Philip, Roshi, The Three Pillars of Zen, Doubleday, 1989.

Kirwan, John, All Blacks Don't Cry, Penguin Books, 2010.

Kolk, Van Der, Bessel, The Body Keeps the Score, Penguin Books, 2015.

Hay, Louise L., You Can Heal Your Life, Hay House, 1991.

Holford, Patrick, New Optimum Nutrition Bible, Piatkus Books, 2004.

2

Lockie, Andrew and Nicola Geddes, Homeopathy: The Principles and Practice of Treatment, RD Press, 1995.

Maher, Suzanne, Spirit, Affirmations Publishing House, 2008.

Mandela, Nelson, The Illustrated Long Walk To Freedom, Little, Brown, 2001.

Roizen, Michael and Mehmet Oz, You: The Owner's Manual, HarperCollins, 2005.

Rosen, Tommy, Recovery 2.0: Move Beyond Addiction and Upgrade Your Life, Hay House, 2014.

Peck, M.Scott, The Road Less Travelled: A New Psychology of Love, Traditional Values and Spiritual Growth, Arrow, 1989.

Pinkney, Maggie (ed.) and Whiter Barbara (ed.), Pocket Positives, Summit Press, 2001.

Sanborn, Mark, The Fred Factor, Random House, 2004.

Sher, Brian, R.Goldman, B. Orgo, You Are Not Crazy, It's Your Hormones!, Redwood Publishing, 2004.

Tolle, Eckhart, The Power of Now, Hachette Australia, 2004.

Urwin, Jack, Man Up, Icon Books, 2016.

Verrier, Nancy, The Primal Wound: Understanding The Adopted Child, Verrier Publishing,1993.

Welton, Kathleen (ed.), The Little Book of Gratitude Quotes, Aka Associates Inc, 2011.

Xue Ren Tze Yuan, Wellbeing Begins With You, Yuan Tze Centre, Wellington NZ, 2015.

Table of Figures

Help... I've lost my emotional freedom... I know it's around here somewhere!

Humans have a beginning and an end, and the stuff in between. So who are you — a product of all the previous stuff? Dorothy Simpson explains in easy-to-understand language how the stuff impacts you. Hurt people unknowingly hurt other people, and this emphasises the roll-on effect of the confusing stuff.

Discover emotional freedom within these pages!

Delivering a fusion of knowledge from psychology, sociology, health care and mysticism — Dorothy shares her story of locating and making peace with her wobbly foundation and finding love, inner calm and belonging.

Identify and break free of the mind game of "Is it me, or is it them who's making me feel bad?"

Gain fresh perspectives and self-mastery of your body and mind.

Find a path to newer, healthier relationships, and a range of self-care options.

ISBN 978-0-473-43459-5

www.ingramcontent.com/pod-product-compliance
Lightning Source LLC
Chambersburg PA
CBHW060932050726
47592CB00003B/915